Preventing Sexual Abuse

Activities and Strategies for Those Working with Children and Adolescents

Second Edition

Curriculum Guides for
K-6, 7-12, and Special Populations

Carol A. Plummer

LP LEARNING PUBLICATIONS, INC.
Holmes Beach, Florida

Library of Congress Number: 83-82306

ISBN 1-55691-114-9

Learning Publications, Inc.
5351 Gulf Drive
P.O. Box 1338
Holmes Beach, FL 34218-1338

Development funded in part by Grant No. 90-CA-817A101 for the National Center on Child Abuse and Neglect; Children's Bureau, Administration for Children, Youth and Families; Office of Human Development Services: U.S. Department of Health and Human Services.

Contributing artwork by Barbara J. Wirtz, and "The Support Tree" by Anthony Plummer-Yoder

Printing: 5 4 3 2 1   Year: 9 8 7

Printed in the United States of America

Contents

"No" • **Art Activities:** Puppets • Warm Fuzzies and Cold Pricklies • Touch Lines • Language Arts Skills • Role Plays • Guidelines for Introducing the Topic • Pre- and Post-Test for Elementary Students • Pre- and Post-Test Answers for Elementary Students • Sample Letters to Parents • "The Warm Fuzzy Story" • Activity Sheets • The Support Tree

Basic Concepts to Communicate to Students • Using the Curriculum and Lesson Plans • Tips for Working with Grades 7–9 • Tips for Working with Grades 10–12 • Five-Day Curriculum Overview • Three-Day Curriculum Overview • One-Day Curriculum Overview • **Five-Day Curriculum:** Lesson 1: The Problem • Lesson 2: Strangers • Lesson 3: Incest • Lesson 4: Acquaintance Rape and Sexual Harassment • Lesson 5: Prevention and Resources • **Three-Day Curriculum:** Lesson 1: Problem Overview • Lesson 2: Focus on Incest • Lesson 3: Focus on Prevention Skills • **One-Day Curriculum:** One-Day Presentation • **Optional Activities:** Saying "No" to Touch • Images of Males/Females/Children • Blaming/Not Blaming the Victim • Community Resources • Role Plays • Middle and High School Pre- and Post-Test • Pre- and Post-Test Answer Key for Middle and High School Students • Victims Panel Exercise • Notes to Secondary Teachers • Case Studies

Preface

This book is for teachers, school counselors, nurses, mental health professionals, residential caretakers, and recreational leaders. In fact, it is for anyone who may have the opportunity to spend time with groups of young people. It is best described as a skeleton outline of a program for assisting you to help youngsters prevent sexual abuse. Because it covers such a wide range of ages and abilities, I have kept it general enough for you to alter to your group's particular level. Thus, many optional activities are given from which to choose. Space for notes and ideas has been added wherever possible and your own pages may be inserted within this text. This guide is a gift I offer to you to use and to improve. More importantly, it is a gift to children both to encourage and to empower them.

Although this book is about child sexual abuse, that problem's relationship to rape and sexual assault deserves to be at least mentioned. A large majority of perpetrators of sexual abuse are men — most victims are women and children. It is common for people to become greatly alarmed by the sexual abuse of children and it is incumbent upon us to prevent and curtail this abuse. However, rapes and assaults of women must be opposed and worked against with equally fervent resolve. As long as this society in any way tolerates the abuse of women by men, the sexual abuse of children will be a logical extension and thus continue. The domination and control by the powerful of those perceived as weak and powerless must end to increase the chances for a more humane society.

Acknowledgments

The following persons were most instrumental in assisting to create this curriculum guide. Many thanks to all of them for their inspiration, feedback, input, corrections, and ideas. Without them, the pages might all still be blank.

Peggy Blocznski	Ethel Metzler
Geraldine Crisci	Mary Metzler
Linda Fortune	Marlys Olson
Carol Gilliom	Sue Plank
Paul Hartman	Donna Polacious
Catharine Higgs	Carla Steiger-Meister
Illusion Theater	Sandy Stern
Cordelia Anderson Kent	Everett Thomas
Bonnie Keyser	Nancy Thompson
Connie Kreider	Oralee Wachter
Wanda Lang	Helen Watts
Nancy Lefever	Darlene Wedge
Judy Little	Don Yost
Kee MacFarlan	

I am indebted to the parents, children, teachers, and administrators who wanted our program and helped us test and improve our materials. These include, among others, Goshen Community Schools, Concord Schools, Elkhart Community Schools, and two exceptionally supportive principals, Bob Duell and Don Wysong.

Special thanks and acknowledgment go to the Bridgework Theater.

I also wish to extend my sincere gratitude to the staff of the National Center on Child Abuse and Neglect (NCCAN) and to the other NCCAN project directors who shared and supported me through the ups and downs.

Barbara J. Wirtz, who was able to enhance and expand all these words with her unique artistic touch and insight, deserves special credit.

For inspiration, support, patience, I thank my son, Anthony. He has tolerated my passion for prevention these past 17 years. Extra special thanks, as well, to the Association for Sexual Abuse Prevention members, especially Cordelia Anderson, Geri Crisci, Pnina Tobin, Elda Dawber, Mary Hall, Rhonda Day, and Alice Ray, for their long-term vision and hard work on behalf of children.

Note from the Author

As Cordelia Anderson of Illusion Theater once stated, "You're not on a headhunt for victims." This program is meant to increase information and skills for students in recognizing child sexual abuse, and avoiding or averting abusive situations. Identifying and promoting local resources available for past or present victims is also an important part of the program. However, it is meant to help prevent sexual abuse from ever happening to the participants. Keep that goal in mind.

If victims are detected through improved teacher alertness or victim disclosures, use your reporting protocol and on-site crisis counselors. While responsibility and sensitivity to victims is essential, our job in prevention is to point children in the direction of services, not provide counseling or do investigation of reports. If services are inadequate, this should be explored at a task force or advisory board level and may necessitate some victim advocacy.

In one school where this curriculum was used, not one child reported past or present abuse immediately following the presentations. Several teachers were concerned about what they had done wrong since they knew there were probably abuse victims in every class.

The teachers had done nothing wrong, but were forgetting the point of preventive education. The point is not to seek out and force victims to get immediate intervention. The primary goal is to expand children's information, power, and resources so that sexual abuse can be prevented from happening. If children learn the definition of sexual abuse, the ways that children typically get tricked or trapped, that sexual abuse is not "normal," such secrets are inappropriate, they have permission to refuse unwanted touch, and have a list of people or agencies that are helpful resources — this achieves the program's goals. When children's options are increased and when they are well-informed, they are most likely to be safe.

The secondary service of this program is to refer victims, at the time they report abuse, to appropriate services in a sensitive and expedient manner. Preoccupation with finding victims is counterproductive. Pushing a child who has kept the silence for years to report because she is fidgety during class may only make her hide the secret more. She deserves the right to disclose to whom and when she wants. The offender has already robbed her of certain rights; we must not make her feel even less powerful by taking away more. Besides, the fidgety child may only need a bathroom break! Do not make hasty assumptions.

Remember as well, that you will have provided a list of people with whom children can share such problems. We cannot know the full impact of our educational input. Perhaps several children told relatives or a pastor. Perhaps other victims are pondering the information and need to gather up the strength to disclose a few months from now. But consider the power of the information shared with children. All the children are more informed, more alert, more aware of dangers and possibilities. Safety is our ultimate goal. We are often simply planting the seeds for prevention and less often reaping the results of our work.

1
Defining the Problem

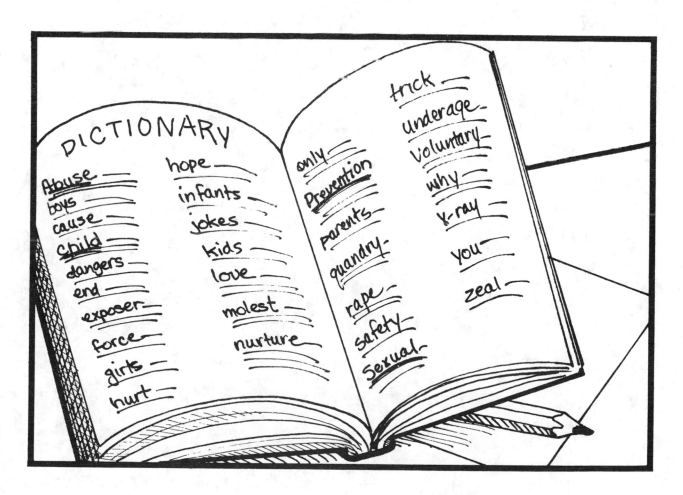

1
Defining the Problem

- Child — A young person between babyhood and youth.

- Sexual — Pertaining to sex.

- Abuse — Mistreatment; misuse; to treat in a harmful, injurious, or offensive way; to commit indecent assault upon.

- Prevention — The act of hindering, obstructing; effective hindrance or obstruction.

How is "Child Abuse Prevention" Defined?

Webster's Dictionary is not necessarily a great help in understanding this particular topic. Who exactly is a child? When does touch become sexual? When does touch become abusive? What is prevention? How can you prove that you're preventing something from happening?

All these are questions I, with the Bridgework Theater staff, had to wrestle with in putting together a "Child Sexual Abuse Prevention" project in 1980 in Goshen, Indiana. All are questions you will need to consider if you choose to work in the field.

For our purposes, a child is considered to be legally defined as one usually age 18 or younger. Sexual abuse is whenever someone is forced or tricked into sexual contact (which could be genital touch, but also includes child pornography or obscene phone calls). Prevention is an active intervention plan comprised of various with the ultimate goal of averting or avoiding a negative outcome, in this case, sexual abuse. Proving prevention is difficult at best and often impossible. However, we can demonstrate an increase in both children's knowledge and skills after using this program.* Linda Sanford argues in *The Silent Children* (1980), and I agree, that a lack of knowledge, skills, and resources sets up children to more likely become victims than those children who are better informed.

Despite a recent backlash questioning its reality or seriousness, sexual victimization of children is a very real problem today in the United States. It ranges from fondling by strangers to incest, from child pornography to child prostitution. As many as 38 percent of all female children will be victims of child sexual abuse before reaching age 18 (Russell 1986). Male children are also at high risk for sexual abuse; one in 11 will become a sexual abuse victim before manhood (Finkelhor 1979). It's a problem we can no longer ignore or avoid.

A variety of theories exist regarding the causes and cures of this problem. Some theories focus on the individual pathology of the offender, the cooperation of the mother in cases of

---

*Numerous studies now document the value of child sexual abuse prevention programs. See Appendix J for a list of studies.

incest, the contribution of the media's sexualization of children, or the entire family's protection of their incestuous "secret." The researchers' data is far from being complete and in any case, agreement on these points may be a long time coming.

Regardless of theories, most educators agree to concentrate on preventing child sexual abuse rather than worry about treatment methods after the fact. The bad news is that we cannot prevent all sexual abuse from happening. In spite of your efforts to teach or protect a child, or the child's efforts to resist or be assertive, the offenders are ultimately responsible and may abuse regardless. However, the good news is that nearly anyone, anywhere can contribute to this prevention effort.

We can do this in two ways:

☑ We, as adults who relate to and care about children, first need to educate ourselves about this serious social problem. All of us need more self-awareness: doctors, nurses, prosecutors, parents, clergy, attorneys, teachers, social workers (and anyone else who has a niece, nephew, or loves a child).

☑ We need to develop ways to share information with and improve skills of children regarding prevention of sexual abuse. Parents, ministers, teachers, doctors, social workers, and others can learn to talk to children sensitively and clearly about this topic.

That's what this curriculum guide is all about — to help you become one of those desperately needed resources for children.

Note: The statistics regarding incidence of and facts about child sexual abuse prevention throughout the book are approximations. The intent is to present generally accepted data in the field rather than to quote specific research studies. For readers who desire more detailed and exact statistical support, the books listed in Appendix J provide adequate documentation.

I have developed my prevention theory enhanced by David Finkelhor's idea that four preconditions must exist in order for sexual abuse to occur. We can intervene in any of the four factors to prevent abuse. The following chart demonstrates the general preconditions and stimulates ideas of many ways we can interfere with potential abuse:

A person has a proclivity for abuse	A person lacks internal controls	A person lacks external controls	A person has access to children
raise healthy, safe children	treat alcohol and drug abuse to reduce impulsivity	establish clear sexual harassment policies in schools and work places	set rules about when and who may enter child-care agencies
provide adequate treatment for past abuse victims	strengthen empathy training in elementary school	pass laws with clear penalties for assaults	screen, train, and monitor all staff who work with children
provide rapid and effective treatment for youthful sex offenders	challenge advertising that sexualizes children	encourage religious and social organizations to send strong messages opposing abuse	carefully select baby-sitters and ask how your children feel about them
			teach children and parents prevention messages

Because it is too easy to burden children unduly with prevention, we must broaden our definition to examine how adults must be involved in prevention. We cannot simply tell children to say "no," than run and tell. We must make those dangerous encounters less and less likely by involvement in all the other levels of prevention. For example, in a school, youth-serving agency, or day-care center, it is important to examine prevention procedures in the following.

- Prevention through the Employment Process

- Prevention through Facility Design

- Prevention through Operational Procedures

Prevention through the Employment Process

1. Criminal background checks.

2. Check all references and past employment. Phone contact preferable to mailed recommendations.

3. Thorough interview process using open-ended questions concerning disciplinary methods experienced in childhood and preferred as an adult, attitudes about recent day-care cases.

4. Express the center's commitment to child abuse prevention and reporting.

5. Establish an orientation and probation period to receive training regarding policies and for observation.

6. Check for gaps in employment history.

7. Note peer interactions — overly focused in personal and professional life on children?

What are some specific policies, procedures, and techniques that you use in your center when hiring staff?

_____

_____

_____

What are some procedures that you would like to see implemented?

_____

_____

_____

_____

Prevention through Facility Design

Considerations:

1. Alarmed entrances (other than front).

2. Concave mirrors.

3. No doors on toilet rooms or on stalls for younger children.

4. Windows in storage room doors.

5. Half-walls, open spaces.

6. Dimmer switches.

7. Bell or chime on entrance.

8. Visible outside areas.

9. Hand-washing fixtures in activity room.

10. Keep closets and storage rooms locked and near the office or classroom. May take doors off storage closets if daily use items are kept inside.

11. Use of intercoms to hear in restrooms.

12. Create "off-base" areas that are clearly understood by children, especially in public buildings.

13. No dead space in the classroom that isn't visible by an adult from a central point.

14. Sinks and drinking fountains in outdoor play area.

15. Visibility from and to outdoors.

16. Separate bathrooms for older children.

17. Note items such as paint brushes, belts, ropes, in places where they don't belong.

What are some specific things you can realistically implement in your center to aid in prevention through facility design?

_____

_____

_____

Prevention through Operational Procedures

Policies to Consider:

1. Staff orientation program.

2. Volunteers (training, monitoring).

3. Disciplinary guidelines. Positive and clear, given both in writing and orally.

4. Non-compliance of staff.

5. Parental access.

6. Staffing and conduct. Suggest two staff present at all times.

7. Release of children.

8. Prevention and education programs.

9. Reporting abuse. Establish protocol and a good relationship with local child protection services.

10. Staff training programs on ongoing basis regarding child abuse prevention, identification, and reporting.

What are some policies in place in your center which aid in the prevention process?

_____

_____

_____

_____

What are some operational procedures you could implement which would aid in prevention?

_____

_____

_____

_____

2
Where Do You Begin?

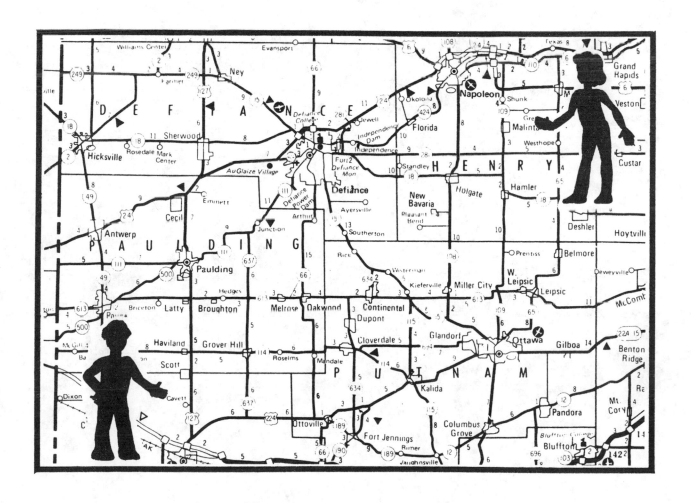

2
Where Do You Begin?

Begin Where You Are!

Prevention programs do not magically appear simply because there is a crying need for them. People become concerned, angry, and frustrated with the atrocity of child sexual abuse and say, "I want to do whatever I can to stop this abuse." Most often, these are people who are the closest to children — parents, teachers, or social workers. There are important roles for all of us in prevention work.

The recommendations and strategies found in this book are based upon my experiences for three years as the director of a sexual abuse prevention program in northern Indiana and since then as a national prevention consultant and trainer. In Chapter 6 you will find curriculum materials used successfully with grades kindergarten through six with adaptations for use with older developmentally disabled students or adults. A curriculum for middle and senior high school students (and in some cases, young adult groups) are detailed in Chapter 7. Whether you duplicate or adapt the materials, they should provide you with helpful resources to "begin where you are" in sexual abuse prevention program development.

Some of you are a part of a school system — a principal, school board member, teacher, superintendent, counselor, or school nurse. You may be wondering how sexual abuse programming can be squeezed into already crowded schedules; if it will dump more work onto busy teachers; how parents respond; how such programs work in other (small town, rural, inner city, conservative, liberal, religious) school systems. You may also wonder what private community agencies in your area already are doing about child sexual abuse.

Others work outside the school system, such as for a local social service agency, a member of a parent or service organization, a physician, judge, public health nurse, or an active community volunteer. Convinced that sexual abuse is a problem, you may question the level of awareness in your community. You may have heard of programs that directly educate school-age children during the school day. Such programs make sense and sound essential — but how do you get schools interested in such a program? Who would teach it? How could you be of help if such a program were based within the public school system? If the schools flat-out refused to develop preventive education, what else could be done? In the next chapter, these concerns will be addressed.

3
Making a Prevention Program Work

3
Making a Prevention Program Work

If you wish to start a prevention program, you may have plans ranging from a one-time presentation for high-schoolers all the way to an ongoing multi-faceted program such as described here. In either case, these guidelines will help you, although they should never be construed as being the only formula that works. Perhaps these suggestions will help you avoid some mistakes I made, but you will discover new mistakes. You will also uncover new techniques — so keep an open mind and keep learning.

If You Are Working Within the School System:

☑ Remember even professionals often need additional information about child sexual abuse. It is typical for a task force or advisory board to spend a period of time on self education before tackling other organizational tasks. Because of a rapidly changing field, even the most sophisticated professionals need ongoing updates and training. Another important objective is to ascertain what is already being done in your community. Check with local agencies which can help you or would be able to put you in touch with whomever could be most helpful.

You will want to find out:

■ What services are there for prevention, intervention, and treatment in your area?

■ Would local agencies support a sexual abuse prevention program in your school? Do they consider it valuable? Have there been previous programs and what reception did they receive?

■ Do they have any resources you could use for successful program implementation? These could include staff time, financial resources, or printed materials, films, or videotapes.

■ Would your work in any way duplicate work that is already underway? If so, how could you plug into and support existing efforts?

■ Has there been any opposition to prevention programming and is it organized? What are the major concerns?

☑ Decide on the scope of your program. If, as a teacher, you wish to add a lesson in your "family life" class on child sexual abuse prevention, you may not need administrative clearance. However, if you do half-hour sessions on the topic for one week with third graders, you will probably need for your principal to be aware and grant permission. Many school systems require "tops down" decisions for curriculum additions. Particularly if you hope to establish a prevention curriculum schoolwide or systemwide, the superintendent, parents, and school board will need to endorse the program. Sometimes special curriculum committees handle these changes, such as a health curriculum committee. As an insider, you are in a good position to know how your school system handles such program adoptions.

☑ If you choose to broaden your scope beyond presentations in your own classroom this year, an advisory board would be recommended. This should be made up of school, community, and agency representatives. An advisory board will:

- assist with decision making

- help promote community support

- assist in raising funds for materials and staff development

- help respond to any community concerns

☑ Once there is a plan with community and school support, it is best to pilot the program with certain targeted age groups or schools. Although other communities have shown significant benefits through evaluation of their programs, you will want to get feedback from your pilot project to help expedite systemwide implementation. Questions which should be asked include:

- Are the children learning?

- Do they learn new information, change attitudes, and improve their skills?

- Do the teachers feel prepared to use the curriculum?

- What exercises worked the best?

- What are parental reactions?

- Do parents or teachers have suggestions?

☑ Ongoing contact with and consultation from outside agencies enhances program implementation. It is especially important to stay connected to child protective services, the unit within the department of public welfare (or social services) responsible for investigation of potential child abuse cases. Frequent teacher inservices can assist in building the school/child protective services relationship. It also keeps teachers aware of their reporting responsibility, thus improving services to children.

☑ Instructors who feel comfortable with the subject matter and who are well-trained and familiar with available teaching resources are critical to the success of any prevention program. Such programs for children have been taught successfully by school nurses, guidance counselors, classroom teachers, social service agency personnel, and community volunteers. A critical consideration at the staff selection and training stage is to choose the person(s) most likely to contribute to the ongoing success of your program.

☑ The issue of funding is bound to arise. Sexual abuse prevention programs can be as elaborate or conservative as you choose. Consider the value of the program as well as which methods are most cost-effective in your situation. Live play presentations in conjunction with classroom exercises listed in this book are expensive, but will be of greater impact upon youngsters. Films and videotapes have an added advantage in that they can be used repetitively on an annual basis. However, simply supplying teachers with curriculum materials such as this book goes a long way toward instructing children about basic personal safety.

Possible sources for funding a sexual abuse prevention program include:

- PTA budgets

- Library budgets

- Assembly program monies (especially for live plays)

- Local or state foundations

- Businesses and industry

- Community service organizations

- Mental health centers

- State funds for child abuse prevention, such as Children's Trust Funds

☑ A good goal for school prevention programs is to design and stick to a system that with minor modifications will work year after year.

Examples:

- Teacher inservices each fall and spring

- Annual letters to parents

- In-class program to second graders using this curriculum in conjunction with the film *No More Secrets* (Appendix J)

- In-class program to fifth graders using this curriculum guide and a live educational play

- In-class presentation to eighth graders using this curriculum guide and *Acquaintance Rape* films or videotapes (Appendix J)

- Ongoing feedback from parents and an advisory board for program improvements.

If You Are Working from Outside the School System:

☑ Develop a task force to promote child sexual abuse prevention locally or countywide. Although such groups may evolve from sexual assault task forces or child abuse prevention committees, it is important to make certain there is a focus on children, child sexual abuse, and on prevention. In committees with a broader scope of interest, there may be a tendency to focus more on treatment modalities, adult rape, or physical child abuse. When possible, begin a new committee focused exclusively on child sexual abuse prevention to avoid such difficulties. Be sure to include school and agency representatives, parents, medical professionals, child protective services representatives and others who can lend valuable resources to such work. Get professional support and backing, but remember that even professionals often need additional information about child sexual abuse. It is typical for a task force or advisory board to spend a period of time on self-education before tackling other organizational tasks. One objective of the task force would be to critique and advocate for better services from all agencies dealing with child sexual abuse.

☑ Begin with community awareness efforts. Community acceptance and cooperation is generally favorable when there is maximum use of community resources and a commitment to not duplicate present services. All forms of the media have demonstrated a willingness to publicize both the facts on the problem of child sexual abuse (especially local statistics) and approaches to preventing it. It pays to be assertive with the media, especially in rural areas or small towns. Be sure to include radio, television, and newspapers, but also reach out via the various community group or church newsletters.

☑ Develop a clear plan of what you want to do, what you realistically can accomplish, and who is responsible for each task. Do not overload yourself or others due to enthusiasm or a sense of urgency. It is better to start with what is manageable and include plans for adding additional services than to have to cut back and become discouraged. Nothing is more discouraging than feeling overwhelmed by unrealistic goals.

☑ Be prepared for questions and criticism. Actually, questions and criticisms are positive signs. They indicate a certain caution and concern about how we educate children. Open communication is easier to deal with than "underground" resistance in the long run. Though you may feel frustrated, remember no one is your enemy. Opponents are probably equally concerned about children. Get the answers and publicize the facts. The facts are what ultimately "sell" people on child sexual abuse prevention. Common concerns are:

- "Our community is already aware of this problem."

  This may be true, but it is not enough to completely eradicate it. Children are the last "front" in stopping child sexual abuse. We owe it to them to give them adequate information to protect themselves from harm.

- "This information is too 'stimulating' for children. They may attempt abusing one another."

It is true that many children play "doctor," regardless of whether or not there is a prevention program. However, experience shows that children take this safety information seriously and rarely see it as "sexy." There is no evidence that they attempt abusing one another. Quite the contrary, they will be better able to protect themselves and/or report such attempts.

■ "The only real prevention is treatment."

While treatment is important, empowering children who remain at risk (while attempting to cure or remove offenders) is only socially responsible behavior. Prevention and treatment programs should ideally work together. However, prevention programs are particularly needed where there are no specific treatment facilities and may even mobilize the development of a specialized treatment program due to a newly perceived need.

■ "We already have other, more important special programs in our schools, such as alcohol or drug abuse prevention."

Child sexual abuse prevention is no more or less important than substance abuse prevention. In fact, studies consistently show links between abused children, substance abuse and crime. Children who abuse alcohol and drugs usually have a reason — often it's to blot out the pain of physical, sexual, or emotional abuse. Additionally, substance abuse by adults occurs in most instances of sexual abuse of children.

☑ The public schools are the one place where most children spend a great deal of time. You will want to generate support for an in-school program at all levels — from teachers, parents, administrators, and guidance counselors to school nurses. Knowing the system and having personal credibility through past contacts or recommendations from a school representative are critical to your chances for being "heard." It will also increase your understanding of their concerns and difficulties in implementing such a program. You want to be as supportive to the school as possible in undertaking this program and, remember, it is ultimately a school program. Administrators are aware they will take any flack resulting from its adoption. Respect their pace and recognize the school's right to make major decisions about implementation. For example, we always have school administrators decide whether or not to send permission slips or informational notes home to parents. Regardless of your personal feelings about parental involvement, some administrators will choose to use permission slips and some will not. It is the school's choice and responsibility to handle the resulting parental response.

☑ Private schools, church youth groups, scout troops, and other youth gathering places are also ideal places to use this curriculum. Implementation in such groups may help to open doors to school systems because of the obvious public support and resulting requests from enthusiastic parents.

☑ Focus on the issue of safety, not sexuality. This program is not sex education and, although it may, it does not need to include it. Providing information, as well as expanding skills and options in potentially dangerous situations are the goals of this program. Many communities use this program although they have never had sex education programs.

- ■ Throughout the years, sex education has been controversial. Some working in prevention programs feel strongly that abuse and sexuality should not be linked, making a child's first "sex education" about "bad touch." Others feel a lack of adequate sex education places children at additional risk of abuse. Your community may or may not struggle with this issue but it need not stop prevention efforts.

☑ The focus needs to constantly be on providing information in a responsible, adequate, and understandable manner to children. In training instructors in the use of plays, scripts, curricula, and videotapes, timing and completeness as well as adequate follow-up services for children should be consistently stressed.

☑ When working with the schools, clarify from the start your commitment to and expectations for guaranteeing that suspicions of abuse are reported. This needs to be balanced, however, with the need to follow school protocol in reporting procedures, when they are, in fact, in operation. Decide who will report abuse cases and make sure someone reports. This is mandated by law in every state. To date, there are no penalties for "good faith" reports, but may be for failure to report.

☑ A child sexual abuse prevention program should facilitate improved communication and rapport between child protective service (CPS) workers and the schools. This can be done through liaison work and training for both groups. It is also helpful to have CPS workers assist in the training of teachers. They are the most knowledgeable about investigative procedures and can become "real people" to school personnel through direct contact. Unfortunately, mistrust is often present between these groups. CPS workers often claim schools do not report abuse and on occasion feel schools harass CPS for information which cannot be legally disclosed. Schools argue that CPS often does not "do anything" when reports are made and won't share any information with the educators who deal closely with the child and family. The rights and responsibilities of both CPS and school personnel need to be well-defined and to be more fully understood by both groups in order to be mutually appreciated.

☑ Educational theater and puppetry has proven to be effective in teaching even small children without traumatization. For older audiences, the stage puts the problem "out there" to be seen and discussed. Theater also makes the issue emotionally powerful and thus "close to home" and believable.

☑ Staff screening and mutual support is essential. You may be in a position to present the program to children yourself or to train teachers or others for the task. Prevention advocates and workers should not use this program to work out their own unresolved victimization. Past victims or survivors may work well in a child sexual abuse prevention program, but not until/unless they have healed somewhat from their pain and can focus on program goals, not personal needs. This work of preventive education can cause stress on staff which may result in staff burn-out. Take care of yourselves and each other so that you can continue to do prevention work. It is OK, even necessary, to sometimes say "NO" to requests or to limit your activities. Assert your boundaries, too.

☑ If you train teachers to use the curriculum, make sure they are not feeling "dumped on." Show them that the program is to their advantage because it will help their students. Assure them that professional backup is available for questions, consultation, and referrals.

☑ It is necessary to adapt this program to local needs and values without "reinventing the wheel." Creating new coloring books, curricula, or videotapes may be a waste of valuable time when good ones are already available. Recognize, however, that local community ownership is needed and adaptations/unique variations may enhance ownership.

☑ In organizing a multi-faceted program with broad community involvement, one person or agency may need to take the first step and provide some leadership. As soon as possible, however, it needs to be "our problem" and "our solution" for maximum community investment.

☑ One caution with the media has to do with their desire to interview a victim or emphasize one "case." While adult survivors who have worked through their abuse can help to promote your program, there are emotional risks to such public exposure. Additionally, the publicity you want regards your prevention innovations, not sensational stories about particular individuals. Take care not to use past victims inappropriately for publicity. Re-victimization of those still in pain needs to be avoided at all cost. Any survivor wanting to take a public stand should be encouraged to carefully consider the risks and benefits with their family, friends, or therapist.

☑ Study the flow chart on page 23. Assess your community's progress. However, don't make assumptions that your community is not ready for prevention. Begin where you are and build upon the unique strengths of your community.

☑ Continue to seek and respond to evaluations of your prevention program. Such responsiveness will insure continued growth to better serve the children and the community.

In recent years, demands for program evaluation and research, on prevention have increased. Try to implement ongoing evaluation of your program. It is wise to also keep abreast of the literature on the effectiveness of child sexual abuse prevention programs.

In Summary

Successful child sexual abuse prevention programs include:

- Maximum community support

- Clarity on goals and scope of the program

- An advisory board or other means for insuring ongoing evaluation and support

- A pilot program

- Well-trained instructors

- Community awareness efforts

- Access to children and youth, preferably via the schools

- Good cooperation between schools and child protective services

- A tasteful focus on safety, not sexuality, in all presentations

- A plan for continued implementation

- A commitment to report suspected child abuse

- Support for program staff or volunteers

- Community ownership of the prevention program

- A program consistently updated based on program evaluations and new research on prevention's effectiveness.

Flow Chart for Program Development*

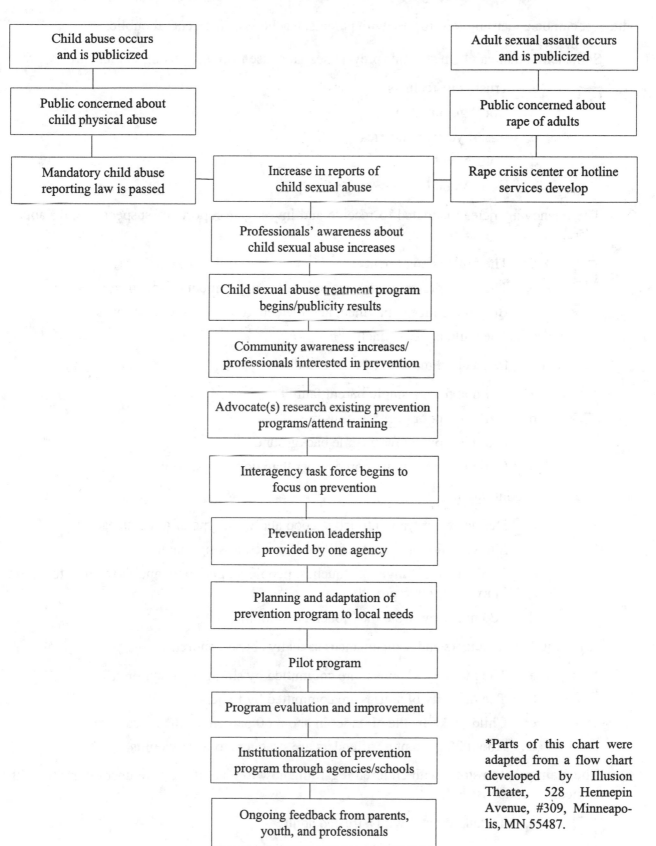

Child abuse occurs and is publicized		Adult sexual assault occurs and is publicized
Public concerned about child physical abuse		Public concerned about rape of adults
Mandatory child abuse reporting law is passed	Increase in reports of child sexual abuse	Rape crisis center or hotline services develop

Professionals' awareness about child sexual abuse increases

Child sexual abuse treatment program begins/publicity results

Community awareness increases/ professionals interested in prevention

Advocate(s) research existing prevention programs/attend training

Interagency task force begins to focus on prevention

Prevention leadership provided by one agency

Planning and adaptation of prevention program to local needs

Pilot program

Program evaluation and improvement

Institutionalization of prevention program through agencies/schools

Ongoing feedback from parents, youth, and professionals

*Parts of this chart were adapted from a flow chart developed by Illusion Theater, 528 Hennepin Avenue, #309, Minneapolis, MN 55487.

Pre- and Post-Test for Adults

This test can be a learning tool for use with parents, teachers, or the general public.

1. Some skills that can help students prevent sexual abuse from happening to them are:

    ☐ a. Trust your feelings
       b. Don't go out alone
       c. Assert your boundaries
       d. Both A and B
       e. Both A and C

2. The agency/agencies mandated to receive and investigate reports of suspected child abuse is/are:

    ☐ a. The police department
       b. The child protective service unit of the department of social services
       c. Both the police department and the department of social services
       d. The child abuse council

3. One indicator that a child may have been sexually abused is:

    ☐ a. Child is from a single-parent family
       b. Child has poor peer relationships
       c. Child is from a low-income background
       d. Child prefers staying home rather than going to school

4. The "touch continuum":

    ☐ a. Defines what type of touch is good and what type of touch is bad
       b. Shows children when to say "no" to a confusing touch
       c. Explains the range of touches people experience and how the touch is individually interpreted
       d. I do not know what the "touch continuum" is

5. Although both strangers and acquaintances sexually abuse children:

    ☐ a. The majority of abuses are committed by strangers to children
       b. The majority of abuses are committed by fathers
       c. Children know the offender in about 60 percent of the cases
       d. About 20 percent of offenders are strangers to their victims

6. The main point to stress with children regarding how to react if they are uncomfortable with someone's touch is:

    ☐ a. To talk about it with a trusted adult

b. To never allow a person to touch their private parts

c. To practice self-defense and use an assertive "yell"

d. To stay away from that person

7. On occasion adults believe that children may lie about sexual abuse. The truth is:

☐ a. Children never lie about sexual abuse

b. Children often under-report cases of sexual abuse or make incidences sound less serious that they are

c. Children often over-report cases of sexual abuse or make incidences sound more serious than they are

8. Sexual abuse is the fault of the victim:

☐ a. Never

b. Only in situations where it happens repeatedly

c. Only when they do not report it because they enjoy the closeness

d. In cases where the adolescent seduces the adults, responsibility is shared

True or False

9. Many delinquent adolescents were sexually abused as children. ☐

10. Much sexual abuse of children involves physical force. ☐

11. Children who have been sexually abused usually tell someone soon after the abuse occurs. ☐

12. Children who are sexually abused often believe they are to blame. ☐

13. Girls who are sexually abused often have poor relationships with their mothers. ☐

14. A professional must have physical evidence of child sexual abuse before reporting the case to the authorities. ☐

15. The majority of sexually abusive adults are male. ☐

16. Seductive behavior in a sexually abused child usually indicates that the child had a major role in initiating the abuse. ☐

17. It is helpful to encourage sexually abused children to forget about the incident as soon as possible. ☐

18. Sexual abuse is more likely to happen in a day-care center than in the child's home. ☐

19. Men should not generally be hired as day-care providers because of the risk that abusive men seek out such positions. ☐

Pre- and Post-Test Answer Key for Adults

1. **e** Both "trust your feelings" and "assert your boundaries" are taught in this program as prevention skills. Limiting the activity of potential victims is not a solution and ultimately restricts freedom while blaming victims if they don't curtail their movement. Trusting intuition when situations feel unsafe and being assertive are both truly helpful in avoiding abusive encounters, however.

2. **c** In the past, child protective services used to investigate all child abuse allegations, however some are now investigated by the police, particularly when the offender is not living with the victim and the caregivers are keeping the child safe from the offender. Where referrals should be made will depend on your state law. If unsure, child protective services can be called and will tell you to whom the report needs to be made.

3. **b** Poor peer relationships frequently result from abusive situations because the child suffers from feeling different from others and may still be trying to keep the secret of their abuse, thus distancing from friendshpis or intimacies. None of the other factors reliably relate to abuse since class status, single parenthood, or religious background does not necessarily increase vulnerability to sexual abuse.

4. **c** The touch continuum is not meant to be a tool for defining what touch is "good" or what touch is "bad," since the experience of touch is a personal one and dependent upon culture, context, and the meaning the child affixes to the touch.

5. **d** In approximately 80 percent of sexual abuse cases the victim knows the offender.

6. **a** Telling an adult is the most reliabile way for a child to get help or guidance if they are uncomfortable with a touch experience. Since a child often does not have the choice of "allowing" or disallowing touch, and self-defense with an adult is often futile and perhaps even counter-indicated, these are not good answers. Avoiding a person will also not ensure safety.

7. **b** Children are far more likely to under-report abuse due to fear of repercussions to themselves or their families or even to the offender, who may be liked for other aspects of their personality.

8. **a** Victims of sexual abuse should never be blamed for the abuse, even if they made unwise choices or forgot to use their prevention guidelines.

9.	T	14.	F
10.	F	15.	T
11.	F	16.	F
12.	T	17.	F
13.	T	18.	F
		19.	F

4
Involving Parents

4
Involving Parents

Generally speaking, the more parents know about this program, which is designed for the safety of their children, the more supportive they are. Naturally, parents will need assurance that their children are being taught about sensitive subject matter in a carefully planned and tasteful manner. Many parents have thanked us for talking to their children because, while they agree the topic is important, some parents feel unsure about how to discuss this concern with their children. While parents do want to have their children aware and safe, they don't want them unduly alarmed or afraid of all touch. Contacts with parents also reassures them that this prevention approach balances discussion of bad or confusing touch with bountiful examples of good, warm touches.

The sample letter on page 79 may be useful for you to send home a week or so before you present the program. Some schools have also sent home permission slips for parents to sign granting or denying permission for their child to participate. The needs of each school vary, but both parent organizations and teachers have expressed concern that high-risk children may be most likely to be denied this essential information. Many principals have explained how an irate parent or two could be handled so that all children could be educated about personal safety. At the junior or senior high level, parental permission is not a major issue.

When Informing Parents, You Have Several Options:

☑ You may invite parents to attend the school presentations with their children. Experience demonstrates that few will actually attend. For working parents this may be impossible. One drawback to inviting parents to attend the presentation is that the presence of adults sometimes distracts from the program or inhibits responses.

☑ You may encourage parents to call the teacher or principal if there are questions or concerns. As with any school program, parents understandably want the door open for their input.

☑ Best of all, you may schedule a special meeting of your school's parent organization in order for parents to hear about the prevention program and preview materials or participate in sample lessons. Parents often want and need additional information about child sexual abuse. They may want to help with prevention efforts but just don't know how.

☑ After the in-class program, send the "Dear Parents" follow-up letter, found on page 80, home with each elementary student. This way, parents can assist in your prevention effort by reinforcing the main program concepts at home. Parents will be happy to know specific ways in which they can help.

In recent years the extent or seriousness of sexual abuse has been the topic of television talk shows and articles in the popular media. Parents may have additional fears due to hearing about false allegations, faulty memory, or adults "coaching" children to make claims. These concerns should be addressed if raised by your familiarity with the relevant literature. Reassurances are appropriate that prevention programs have not been found to promote such outcomes but are geared to prevent abuse from ever happening.

It is usually safe to expect parental support rather than resistance for sexual abuse prevention programs. When they are informed and involved, many parent organizations not only endorse but will financially support such education. It is important, however, to be prepared to answer all questions and criticisms in a straightforward manner which respects parents' interest in their children's welfare.

5
Guidelines for Instructors

5
Guidelines for Instructors

As with all subject matter, this topic will be taught best by those who are thoroughly familiar and comfortable with the material. Adequate training or self-instruction is critical to the success of these units. Many workshops on abuse awareness are now available.

For the Classroom Teacher Working Independently

First, skim through the entire book. Then carefully read the sections most applicable to the students you will be teaching. This book is designed to be comprehensive yet usable even for those who have little or no background and training in the area of sexual abuse prevention. Close attention to these curriculum guides will help you succeed in your efforts. Soon you will be able to add modifications of your own to better tailor and enrich the lessons to meet your students' needs.

For the Visiting Instructor: Preparing the Staff

As a visiting instructor who will be working in the classrooms of a particular building, you will want to spend some time (at least one half-hour) with staff members to inform them both about the problem and the curriculum you plan to use. Often this can be done just before or just after school in a staff meeting. Because time will be limited, it is helpful to distribute printed materials which will reinforce concepts presented.

Useful hand-outs include:

- Sexual Abuse Fact Sheet (Appendix B)

- Incest Indicators (Appendix G)

- Reporting Guidelines (Appendix H)

- What Happens When a Report is Made (Appendix I)

- Resources for Sexual Abuse Prevention (Appendices J and K)

Commonly asked questions you should be prepared to answer may include:

- "What are you going to do in my classroom?"

- "What are the local and national statistics on this problem?"

- "How will parents be involved?"

- "What will we do with children if their parents won't let them attend prevention sessions?"

- "What should I do if a child reports he or she is being abused?"

- "When and to whom do I report suspicions of child sexual abuse?"

First, make teachers aware that sexual abuse is a problem of local and national scope and briefly share what you plan to do. Then, it is helpful to draw the Touch Continuum on the board for them, show a portion of a film or videotape, or bring copies of this book for their examination. Take care to explain scheduling procedures as well as plans for informing and involving parents. Library time is usually given to those few students who are not permitted to attend the presentation(s). Sometimes alternative films on another health or safety topic are presented so that the children who are not permitted to participate do not feel penalized or stigmatized.

Although teachers need not fear an immediate barrage of children reporting abuse, there may well be new reports. Research shows that reports have occurred as a result of prevention programs and earlier help for victims may be an additional benefit of prevention programs. Familiarize each teacher with school reporting protocol and their legal responsibilities. Describe support systems available during the reporting process both from within and outside the school. For example, the principal or school nurse may confer with the teacher on a suspected case. They may then take joint responsibility for the referral. A therapist or CPS worker may be available for phone consultation if problems or questions arise. It is very important for teachers to be aware of such backup resources. Sometimes teachers are dissatisfied with the actions of CPS, the courts, or therapists, and in some communities these services are not good. However, teachers must still report and demand better services through advocacy efforts if necessary. A handout about this school's protocol could be especially helpful.

For the Trainer of Classroom Teachers

If you are training others to do the actual classroom presentations, more training time is necessary. All of the above material must be covered in addition to more specific "how to" training. A minimum of two to four hours training time (in one to four sessions) should be allotted.

The following is an outline of a typical instructor training session:

Step 1   Make introductions and state the goals for the training session.

Step 2   Present a general overview of the problem of child sexual abuse.

Step 3   Explain prevention goals and philosophy.

Step 4   Distribute copies of the book to each instructor.

Step 5   Walk participants through a sample lesson from the book.

Step 6   "Teach" one or two lessons as though the instructors were the students.

Step 7   Have the teachers ask you the questions they are most afraid of getting from students. Model appropriate responses.

Step 8   Set up exercises in which teachers can practice at their grade level using other participants for feedback. You may want to split the group into smaller groups.

Step 9   Choose several "optional activities" and explore ways they could be used to replace or expand part of a lesson plan.

Step 10   Clarify child sexual abuse reporting protocol and guidelines for when to report. It is very useful to have a child protective services caseworker available for questions at this point in the training. Not only are questions answered accurately, but also such a session builds rapport between the school and the agency.

Step 11   Describe the local resources available to school personnel when questions or concerns arise from this program. When possible, provide names and phone numbers to insert in each of the instructor's books.

Step 12   Let teachers know when and where you are available for further consultation regarding program implementation.

You will probably modify the outline suggested here to meet your own particular needs. However you structure the training, be sure to stress the following essentials:

■   Child sexual abuse is a real problem.

■   The focus of the program is prevention, not treatment. (Referrals will be made to appropriate treatment facilities.)

■   Familiarity and comfort with the curriculum materials is necessary for instructors.

■   Provide opportunities for teachers to practice their new skills before working with students.

■   Clarify how, when, and where to report child abuse.

List backup services available from other agencies and individuals. When possible, leave local support agencies' brochures. Keep in mind there will be past victims and those who know victims in your training session, making knowledge of local resources important not only professionally, but perhaps also personally.

Special Concerns Instructors May Have

Deep down, we probably do not want any child we know to tell us they are or ever were victims of child sexual abuse. As uncomfortable as the topic may make us feel, we need to know about this problem, know our responsibilities in terms of the problem, and help advocate for preventative and therapeutic services for the victims of child sexual abuse.

When working with young people, keep yourself open so that children find you accessible and attentive. On the other hand, do not go hunting behind every bush for a child sexual abuse victim.

What If a Child Reports Abuse During Class?

Step 1   The concern that a child may disclose abuse during class is common — Don't panic! Keep in mind that when a child reports in front of the class it is usually a past abuse that was also reported to some other adult and was somewhat resolved in the past. I have never known an adolescent to disclose an ongoing unreported situation in class. Being able to talk about it would typically indicate that some time has passed and some healing has occurred.

Step 2   Even if it appears to be a current problem, resume the lesson after acknowledging the comment and relating it to the lesson. "Did you tell a grownup, Sharon? Great! It's always important to tell someone you trust, someone who's big enough to help, right?" Generally young people would share such information as would adults — privately with a teacher or counselor.

Step 3   Meanwhile, keep the lesson moving along while allowing for some questions or comments. Avoid, however, long drawn-out stories (which eventually everyone in an elementary classroom will have) about weird phone calls or strangers in cars.

Step 4   Talk to the disclosing child privately at your earliest opportunity. Find out if the problem is indeed current and ongoing. Consult with the appropriate school staff and CPS caseworkers to see if the problem needs to be further investigated.

Step 5   Reinforce and praise the child for telling you about the problem and stress that he or she is not to blame. Don't promise to keep it a secret or that you will save them from pain or hassle. You cannot make such guarantees. Do promise that you will assist them in getting help by telling others who know what to do.

Step 6   If a child feels comfortable enough to share about abuse in front of the whole class, he or she will rarely be breaking down or disruptive during the lesson. However, you should plan to have additional help available should the need arise.

What Can I Do Once a Sexual Abuse Report Is Made?

If a child has reported abuse to you, your most important step (and responsibility by law) is to report the situation to child protective services, the agency mandated to investigate such cases. If upon disclosure you have . . .

- demonstrated your belief in what the child has shared,

- reassured the child you will assist them in getting help,

- emphasized that the problem is not the child's fault, and

- praised the child for reporting

. . . you have already made a large contribution.*

Now that CPS is handling the investigation and providing services to the child and/or the family — what can you do in your role as the child's teacher?

☑ You are not the child's therapist. After sensitively handling the initial disclosure, others such as school social workers, private therapists, or agency counselors should work with the child. Trust their expertise and cooperate in every way possible. If for any reason you are concerned about the services the child is receiving, call CPS again. However, keep in mind that what they are legally permitted to share with you is limited due to confidentiality laws.

☑ Provide as normal and supportive an environment as you can in the classroom. School may seem to be the only safe place for this child, particularly in cases of incest.

☑ Be ready to listen but do not pry. Recognize and reinforce the child's sense of worth with praise and by creating opportunities for success both socially and academically.

☑ You need not avoid all touch but ask for permission first. It's important for the child to know that all touch is not bad and that in this case it indicates warmth and support from you. However, as in all cases of touch, it is important to be certain the interactions are public and clearly appropriate.

What If a Child Lies about Abuse?

I have often been asked if children lie about sexual victimization after being involved with a sexual abuse prevention curriculum such as this. Although there are always exceptions, not one child I have worked with in over 22 years in social service settings has lied or exaggerated to "frame" a disliked adult as a result of prevention input. Misrepresentation is more likely to take the form of not telling parts of the story, downplaying or distancing the situation such as, "It only

---

*Cordelia Anderson has developed the "BASER" model, which may help you remember how to respond: B - Believe the child. It is not your job to decipher credibility. A - Assure the child that it was good to tell you. S - Support the child now and in whatever process ensues. E - Empower the child to get help. R - Refer the matter to the appropriate authorities.

happened once," or "It happened to this friend of mine." Generally children will choose something less embarrassing to themselves if they decide to lie. If, on the rare occasion a child would lie about this, ask more questions because that child also clearly needs special help and attention.

Certainly, children can lie about sexual abuse or anything else. Yet there is no reason to believe that they lie more frequently about sexual abuse, except to deny it, despite current popular notions to the contrary. Most importantly, remember that it is not your job to be an expert on the veracity of reports. Fortunately child protection or mental health experts or even a court of law ascertains that matter. Stay focused on creating a supportive environment so the child can report, however incredible or unlikely the initial fragments of their story may be. Further investigation by trained professionals will later sort out issues of truthfulness, so you can focus on your role of support and referral.

6
Curriculum and Lesson Plans: For K-6 and the Developmentally Disabled

6
Curriculum and Lesson Plans:
For K-6 and the Developmentally Disabled

Basic Concepts to Communicate to Students

- Touch can be good, bad, or confusing.

- If a touch feels bad or confusing it is a good idea to talk to a grownup about it.

- Everyone needs good touches.

- It is OK to say "no" to touch we do not like.

- Child sexual abuse is when children are forced or tricked into touch/sexual contact.

- No one has the right to touch our private parts when we do not want them to.

- It is important to tell a trusted adult if we ever experience sexual abuse.

- We can use personal or community resources and support systems to help us solve any kind of problem.

- Victims are never to blame for sexual abuse.

Using the Curriculum and Lesson Plans

On page 46 is an overview for a five-day presentation and on page 47 is the overview for a three-day unit. (The numbers you see in parentheses in the curriculum overviews refer you to pages where further guidelines on the use of that activity are provided.) Turn to page 48 for daily lesson plans for five days or to page 58 for daily lesson plans for the three-day program. Look over the objectives, materials needed, and the lesson outline. Which activities would your students most enjoy? Which activities would have the greatest potential for learning new skills? How much time can you spend? Which materials do you have access to? Transfer some activities, if desired, from one day to another or from the five-day to the three-day program. Add others from the "Optional Activities" section that immediately follows. Good luck. There will — not surprisingly — be surprises. Our experience has shown, however, that these sessions will be as enjoyable as they are important.

This section of the book gives an outline for presentation to students from kindergarten through grade six, and adaptations for developmentally disabled adults. Because of the wide age range, and ability level, teachers will need to choose which activities and what length of time are most appropriate. Some of our findings may help you in making those determinations. However, teachers tend to be the real experts on what will work best with their students.

Tips for Working with Grades K-3

☑ Ground rules are particularly important to clarify expectations and keep order, particularly if there is the added excitement of an outside speaker.

☑ Role plays do not generally work as well as puppets with this age group. Role plays require more acting skills, movement, and the taking on of a role. However, they need not be ruled out completely, with the older students especially in classrooms where children have done role plays before.

☑ As a rule, spend less time per session, but return to the topic more often. Fifteen to 30 minutes per day for five days is better than 45 to 60 minutes for three days.

☑ A letter home to parents or a meeting to prepare parents is good for building parental support, awareness, and reinforcement of program concepts. (See sample letter, page 79.)

☑ Longer exercises should be omitted. (For example, making Warm Fuzzies or collages.)

☑ Give only a little information each day and repeat the important points frequently. Review briefly at the beginning of each day what was covered in the previous session.

☑ Keep words and definitions simple.

☑ Directly involve as many children as possible — let them answer questions, operate puppets, etc.

☑ Ask for feedback often to make sure concepts and terms are clearly understood.

Tips for Working with Grades 4-6

☑ The seriousness of the topic will have to be addressed immediately. Children are not used to adults saying anything regarding "sex" to them. There may be initial nervousness or embarrassment, often even more than with younger children. One simple way to address the giggling or nervousness is to simply state, "This topic may make us laugh because we're embarrassed, right? But it's important to remember this is a serious problem, not a problem we would consider to be funny if it happened to our friends or to ourselves."

☑ Children will be eager for this information; so curious that they may ask questions about things that seem related to them. I have had questions about dating, pregnancy, and birth control, for example. Do not allow the issues to get confused; answer briefly and bring them back to the topic at hand. However, it is best if you are not too evasive — if you have a sex education program or other school guidelines, deal more in-depth with these issues later. Be certain you know about your school's policy regarding dissemination of sex education. If you are not permitted to answer certain questions, refer them to the school nurse or their parents.

☑ The program can be adequately covered in three days, although there are plenty of materials and content for five days and a longer program is preferable. One day is inadequate and unfair to this age group.

☑ Role plays are most effective to help children build skills that can be used in potentially dangerous situations. Role plays take children one step beyond acquiring knowledge   to practicing it — and are fun to do.

☑ During the instruction period, you may wish to place a special container somewhere in the room to hold written questions from children who are for some reason uncomfortable speaking before the group. This can encourage participation for even the quiet or the bashful student. Answer these anonymous questions during the next class session.

☑ Keep as many children as possible actively involved in role plays, discussion, and other activities.

☑ Make sure you give at least one hand-out for the children to take home, such as one of the coloring sheets on pages 85 and 87. Suggest they discuss the topic with their parents or other significant adults.

Tips for Working with Developmentally Disabled Persons

Developmentally disabled children and adults are at increased risk for sexual victimization. In one study conducted at a local association for the disabled revealed that over half of the developmentally disabled females aged 18–40 (a total of 53 women) had been molested or raped in the past and had been threatened to never tell anyone. Such individuals are at risk for one or more of the following reasons:

- They do not understand what is happening.

- They cannot adequately express themselves, either to report abuse or to stop it.

- They have special needs for attention and affection, increasing their vulnerability.

- They are less likely to be believed if they make a report.

- They are more likely to believe threats or be tricked.

- Information which explains sexuality and contrasts it with sexual abuse has not been given to them.

- Self-reliance is decreased due to the disability. Reliance on authority figures fosters a great deal of obedience to others.

- Offenders sometimes target developmentally disabled persons for all of the above reasons.

Because of the special needs and abilities of developmentally disabled persons, these guidelines are suggested:

☑ Keep things simple. Stay within the range limits of abilities and attention spans of class members.

☑ Be repetitive to reinforce the learning.

☑ Utilize movement, for example, with role plays or cooperative games. Try to keep the active in activities.

☑ Focus on the concrete, not the abstract. Use illustrations that could happen to them. For example, a roommate at their group home who keeps making attempts to touch their private parts when they do not like it.

☑ Use role plays to build skills through practice, rather than relying upon direct instruction. Again, provide examples: "What could you do if your teacher or work supervisor tried to touch your private parts or make you touch theirs?"

☑ Students will not be frustrated if tasks and information are provided at their level of skill and understanding.

☑ It is especially important to emphasize that many touches, and many sexual expressions, can be good. For adults in particular, who may have been treated as asexual (when appropriate sexual expression is never allowed or even discussed), sexual abuse is more likely to occur, even between developmentally disabled persons. Sex education can help to prevent sexual abuse of this population.

☑ Keep the groups small. A one-to-four staff/student ratio is preferable.

☑ Involvement of parents and staff/teachers is crucial for additional reinforcement and support.

☑ Initial ideas of this population about how to respond if being abused are often violent and quite unrealistic. Help the students focus on realistic ways to act.

☑ Developmentally disabled persons are more likely than others to share their own experiences of abuse. While the group will probably be sympathetic and caring, it is best not to focus too long on abuse stories. Relate it to the topic and move on. Make sure that you follow up after the session with individual attention to persons who have shared abuse experiences.

☑ Treat adult developmentally disabled adults as adults. Avoid the "childish" activities.

Five-Day Curriculum Overview

Day 1: All Kinds of Touch	Day 2: Touches We Usually Like	Day 3: Touches We Don't Like or Confuse Us	Day 4: Some Touches Are Against the Rules/Sexual Assault	Day 5: Saying "No" to Touch
1. Introduce topic (76)* 2. Establish ground rules (48) 3. Explain touch continuum (155) • Make touch lines (67) • Role plays on good touch (69-75) 4. Teach one cooperative game (64-65) 5. Questions and answers	1. Review touch continuum (155) • Role plays (69-75) • Practice with puppets (66) 2. Touch match-up exercise, Activity Sheet #2 (87) 3. List times when usually good touch can be bad • unexpected • from strangers • wrong place • wrong time 4. Explore ways to say "no," stress the right to say "no" • Use Options Chart (157) 5. Questions and answers	1. Review previous lessons, focusing on bad, confusing, and no touch 2. Distinguish between good and bad feeling touch (perhaps with collages) 3. Strangers • Review safety rules children know and add to them • Play "What If . . .?" game (66) with primarily strangers as the aggressor 4. Stress child is not to blame • Do Options Chart (157) with stranger situation 5. Questions and answers	1. Review 2. Definitions (153) • Victim/offender • Sexual assault/abuse 3. Ways offenders trick or trap children (discuss or role play) • Bribe • Threat/scare • Confuse 4. Not all offenders are strangers • Use Options Chart (157) with friend/relative as offender 5. Word Bank (68) • Teacher reads about abuse or potential danger, then children write or tell the ending 6. Questions and answers	1. Review definitions (153) 2. Teach prevention skills (159) • Trust your feelings • Be aware • The right to say "no" 3. Role plays (69-75) on being assertive 4. Who can you tell? • Film (171-173) • List resources: personal and community (160) 5. Role Play 1 (71) • If first person told doesn't believe or isn't helpful, tell another and another 6. Coloring sheet (85)/Support Tree (89) 7. Questions and answers
Optional:	**Optional:**	**Optional:**	**Optional:**	**Optional:**
1. Pre-test (77) 2. Use shoe box on teacher's desk for written questions that can be answered the next day	1. Teach another cooperative game (65) 2. Read "Warm Fuzzy Story" (83) 3. Make Warm Fuzzies (67)	1. Tape record story in activity center for children to finish with their new skills 2. Continue use of puppets for practicing	1. Teach another cooperative game to emphasize much touch is good 2. Reporting skills exercise (64)	1. Post-test (77) 2. Test learning with puppets 3. Hand out crisis hotline cards (older children only) 4. Role play calling crisis hotline 5. Review throughout the year

*( ) Indicates cross reference to related page number.

Note: Using puppets works best at the lower elementary level, whereas role plays generally work best for developmentally disabled and older elementary students.

Three-Day Curriculum Overview

Day 1: Touches

1. Introduce topic – include safety, privacy, our senses, crime, and problem solving (76)*
2. Establish ground rules (58)
3. Discuss types of touch and how they make us feel. Draw touch continuum on blackboard (155)
   - Make touch lines (67)
   - Role Play options (69-75)
4. "Warm Fuzzy Story" (83)
5. Teach a cooperative game for "good touch," other excuses to touch, we all need touch (64)
6. Questions and answers

Optional:

1. Do pre-test (77)
2. Exchange Warm Fuzzies – write on heavy paper on other children's backs (67)
3. Use posters

Day 2: Touches We Don't Like or Confuse Us

1. Review previous day
2. Some kinds of touch are against the rules. Definitions (153)
   - Victim/offender
   - Assault/abuse
3. Differentiate good touch from confusing touch
   - Lists (or collages) of good and bad touch
   - Touch match-up exercise. Activity Sheet #2 (87).
   - Stress that both victim and offender can be anyone
4. Safety with strangers
   - List rules children know
   - Use Options Chart (157)
5. Who does these crimes? It can be friends, family, grownups you know
6. Questions and answers

Optional:

1. Use posters
2. Role play (69-75)
3. Use Hula Hoops to express personal boundaries (61)

Day 3: Options for Help

1. Brief review
2. Introduce three prevention skills (159)
   - Trust your feelings
   - Be aware of what's around you
   - You have the right to say "no"
3. Use Options Chart (157) with prevention skills
4. Practice saying "no" with role plays or puppets
5. View films *No More Secrets* or *Who Do You Tell?* (172, 173)
6. List resources (160)
   - Personal
   - Community
7. Coloring sheet (85) or Support Tree (89)

Optional:

1. Do post-test (77)
2. Use posters
3. Role plays (69-75)
4. Pass out crisis hotline cards to older children
5. End with good touch or cooperative game (64)

*( ) Indicates cross reference to related page number.

Lesson 1: All Kinds of Touch

Objectives:

1.   To establish ground rules for a serious discussion.

2.   To clearly introduce the topic for types of touch and how they can make us feel.

3.   To demonstrate that not all touch is bad by playing one cooperative game with children.

4.   To encourage practice of skills through role plays or personal touch lines.

By end of presentation students will:

■   List ground rules.

■   Describe three or more types of touch on the touch continuum.

■   Make a personal touch line or participate in role plays about good touch.

■   Play one cooperative game with the group.

Materials Needed: Blackboard, paper, pencils, crayons

Prerequisites: None

Length of Activity: 20-45 minutes

Age: 6-12

Size of Group: Maximum of 30

Suggested Groups: Elementary or developmentally disabled

Outline of Presentation: "All Kinds of Touch"

1.   Introduce topic comfortably using the guidelines on page 76.

2.   Establish ground rules for discussion.

■   It's sometimes hard or embarrassing to talk about these things.

■   No put-downs.

■   Take turns talking or raising hands to speak.

3. Introduce the touch continuum.

   ■ Draw the touch continuum on blackboard — include feelings associated with various touches.

   ■ Make personal touch lines.

   ■ Do role plays on good-feeling touch with children who volunteer.

4. Teach one cooperative game.

   ■ Emphasize we all like good touches.

   ■ We all have fun.

   ■ No one loses.

   ■ Cooperation is central.

   ■ Some touch makes us feel good.

5. Questions and answers.

Optional:

1. The preparatory letter is sent home to parents one week prior to presentation.

2. Administer the pre-test.

3. Place a container on the teacher's desk for questions to be answered the next day. It can be used throughout the week.

Lesson 2: Touches We Usually Like

Objectives:

1. Review the concepts taught in Lesson 1, communicate range of types of touches and the feelings or responses to them.

2. Stress that each person experiences touch differently, based on place, time, culture, and family.

3. Introduce sensitive but clear ways to say "no" to touch.

By end of presentation students will:

■ Observe or participate in role plays (or use puppets) about touch. List several ways to say "no" to a request.

■ Personalize experiences of touch by use of a touch match-up exercise.

■ Make warm fuzzy balls, describe differences between warm fuzzies, cold pricklies, and fake fuzzies (optional).

Materials needed: Blackboard, touch match-up sheets (Activity Sheet #2) for each child, yarn, scissors, cardboard, sheet, light for shadow puppets or hand puppets (optional).

Prerequisites: Lesson 1 (Five-Day Curriculum)

Length of Activity: 20-45 minutes

Age: 6-12

Size of Group: Maximum of 30

Suggested Groups: Elementary or developmentally disabled

Outline of Presentation: "Touches We Usually Like"

1. Review touch continuum.

    ■ Role plays, or

    ■ Practice with puppets to demonstrate touches.

2. Give each child a touch match-up exercise to complete and color.

3. List on the board the times when a usually good touch can become bad from children's suggestions:

- When unexpected.

- When from a stranger.

- When at the wrong place.

- When at the wrong time.

4. Explore and stress the right ways to say "no."

- Assertive ways attempt not to hurt other's feelings, but respect one's feelings.

- Use Options Chart.

- Use the example of saying "no" to the teacher. Can you ever do this? When and how?

- Stress the right of control over own body especially with touch. For example, "Go jump in a lake." (Would you jump in a lake if I told you to do so?)

5. Questions and answers.

Optional:

1. Teach another cooperative game.

2. Read "Warm Fuzzy Story."

3. Make Warm Fuzzies art project. (This is a time-consuming activity, approximately 30 minutes.)

Lesson 3: Touches We Don't Like or Confuse Us

Objectives:

1. Review previous lessons briefly.

2. Discuss distinguishing types of touch.

3. State safety rules for strangers and expand options for responding.

4. Emphasize that the child is not to blame if approached or bothered.

By end of presentation students will:

- Make group collages about good touch *v.* bad touch (optional).

- List rules about who strangers are and safety precautions to use with them.

- Play the "What if . . .?" game.

- State at least two options for responding to a stranger approaching.

Materials Needed: Blackboard, magazines, scissors, glue, cardboard

Prerequisites: Lesson 2 (Five-Day Curriculum)

Length of Activity: 20-45 minutes

Age: 6-12

Size of Group: Maximum of 30

Suggested Groups: Elementary (or developmentally disabled)

Outline of Presentation: "Touches We Don't Like or Confuse Us"

1. Brief review of previous lessons, focus on touch that feels confusing or bad.

2. Discuss: What is a good touch to you? What is a bad touch to you?

    - Make two collages as a group — one shows good touch between people — one shows bad or confusing touch between people.

    - All answers are "right," based on personal experience, depending on how it makes a person feel.

3. Strangers*

   ■ Who is a stranger? Why do people warn children about strangers? Because people we don't know could hurt a child's feelings or body — and not be safe.

   ■ List rules children know about strangers.

   ■ Add suggestions for responding on the blackboard.

   ■ Play "What if . . .?" game focusing on strangers as aggressor and for practice with role plays or puppets.

4. Stress the child is not to blame

   ■ Use Option Chart with primarily stranger situations. Be sure to emphasize:

      ◆ asking adults in charge for permission to go anywhere

      ◆ not letting others know you are home alone

      ◆ using a buddy to accompany you

      ◆ only speaking to strangers if with an adult (like parents)

      ◆ the rules don't mean all strangers are "bad"

   ■ Stress no one wants to be tricked or trapped into touch.

5. Questions and answers.

Optional:

1. Tape record story in activity center for children to finish with their new skills, additional options.

2. Continue use of puppets to act out situations and solutions.

---

*Defining a "stranger" is a critical aspect of this lesson. A stranger is someone the child doesn't know, even if they have seen the person before (store clerk, neighbor). A stranger could be the friend of a friend or claim to know your parents. Children should not go with strangers, even if they look like a police officer or store security guard unless they have asked the adult who is in charge of them (parents, babysitter, teacher).

Lesson 4: Some Touches Are Against the Rules/Sexual Assault

Objectives:

1. Define sexual assault/abuse terms.

2. Explain ways children are often tricked or trapped into touch or danger.

3. Expand definitions of offender to include not just strangers but also other people the children may know.

By end of presentation students will:

■ Match definitions with words about sexual assault.

■ List two ways offenders trick or trap children.

■ Explore options for action when offender is a friend or relative.

■ Write a creative ending to a story with a vocabulary word bank.

Materials needed: Blackboard, magazine picture of people, puppets (optional)

Prerequisites: Lessons 1, 2, 3 (Five-Day Curriculum)

Age: 6-12

Size of Group: Maximum of 30

Suggested Groups: Elementary or developmentally disabled

Outline of Presentation: "Some Touches Are Against the Rules/Sexual Assault"

1. Review

2. Discuss and clarify definitions with children.

    ■ Safety rules

    ■ Victim/Offender

    ■ Sexual Assault/Abuse

3. Demonstrate ways offenders trick or trap children (using puppets or role plays)

- Bribe

- Threaten/Scare

- Confuse (act nice, then change)

- Say are "teaching" them

- Say the child made it happen (by what they wore or by "wanting" it)

4. Stress that not all offenders are strangers. Use the Options Chart and focus on friends or relatives.

5. Make a word bank.

- List new words on board.

- Tell a story to children of potential abuse.

- Have children complete the story using the new vocabulary words.

  - in a creative writing assignment, or

  - in an oral report.

6. Questions and answers

Optional:

1. Teach another cooperative game to emphasize much touch is good.

2. Do Reporting Skills exercise.

- Describe a person from a magazine picture.

- Have a person enter and exit the room on a pretense of a mission, then 15 minutes later have the children describe the person.

Lesson 5: Saying "No" to Touch

Objectives:

1. Review definitions.

2. Explain prevention skills and show assertive ways to respond to situations.

3. Give children options for people to tell if they are bothered by a problem.

4. Stress reporting to a second or third person if the first one told is not helpful or won't believe them.

By end of presentation students will:

■ List three prevention rules.

■ Practice assertive behaviors through role plays.

■ List three personal and three community resources to help them with problems.

Materials Needed: Blackboard, coloring sheets for each child, or Support Tree Exercise; *No More Secrets, Who Do You Tell?* or other film, projector; crisis hotline cards (optional)

Prerequisites: Lessons 1, 2, 3, 4 (Five-Day Curriculum)

Length of Activity: 20-45 minutes

Age: 6-12

Size of Group: Maximum of 30

Suggested Groups: Elementary or developmentally disabled

Outline of Presentation: "Saying 'No' to Touch"

1. Review definitions/earlier discussions.

2. List prevention skills on the board, with examples:

    ■ Trust your feelings

    ■ Be aware of things and people around you, where you are, your "environment."

    ■ You have the right to say "no" to touch — your body belongs to you.

3. Role plays on being assertive.

4. Who do you tell?

    ■   Show the films *No More Secrets,* or *Who Do You Tell?* (see Bibliography for other films)

    ■   Have each child make a list of personal and community resources.

5. Do Role Play 1, if first person isn't helpful, tell another and another.

6. Coloring Sheet or Support Tree

7. Questions and answers

Optional:

1. Post-test.

2. Test learning with puppets.

3. Hand out crisis hotline cards (older children only).

4. Role play calling crisis hotline.

5. Review and repeat concepts often through the year.

Lesson 1: Touches

Objectives:

1. To introduce the topic in a comfortable manner.

2. To discuss various types of touch and encourage self-awareness regarding how they make children feel.

3. To establish ground rules for discussion.

By end of presentation students will:

- List three types of touch on the touch continuum.

- Play one "good touch" game.

Materials needed: Blackboard, warm fuzzies and cold pricklies (optional)

Prerequisites: None

Length of Activity: 20-45 minutes

Age: 6-12

Size of Group: Maximum of 30

Suggested Groups: Elementary or developmentally disabled

Outline of Presentation: "Touches"

1. Introduce topic in a comfortable manner.

- This is a safety issue.

- Privacy is everyone's right.

- Touch is one of our senses.

- As part of a discussion about crime.

- Learning how to solve difficult problems.

2. Establish ground rules.

- Sometimes it is hard or embarrassing to talk about touch.

- No put-downs.

- Take turns talking or raising hands to speak.

3. Draw touch continuum on blackboard.

- Help children to make their own touch line.

- Children can volunteer to role play types of touch they suggest or use puppets.

4. Read "Warm Fuzzy Story."

5. Stress that we all need good touch. Teach one cooperative game.

- Not all games need a winner and a loser.

- We can all feel good about touch.

6. Questions and Answers.

Optional:

1. Do pre-test.

2. Exchange warm fuzzies — write on heavy paper on other children's backs.

3. Use posters.

Lesson 2: Touches We Don't Like or Confuse Us

Objectives:

1. To define touches that make us feel bad or confused.

2. To brainstorm with children ways to be safe around others.

3. To emphasize safety with strangers, but that not all people who break touching roles are strangers. List some touches that are against the rules (including those touches to private parts of our bodies).

By end of presentation students will:

- Define sexual abuse.

- List three options for safety if endangered by a stranger.

- Make a picture collage of good and bad touches (optional).

Materials Needed: Blackboard, old magazines, glue, scissors, poster board, touch match-up sheets (Activity Sheet #2) for each child.

Prerequisites: Lesson 1 (Three-Day Curriculum)

Length of Activity: 20-45 minutes

Age: 6-12

Size of Group: Maximum of 30

Suggested Groups: Elementary or developmentally disabled

Outline of Presentation: Touches We Don't Like or Confuse Us

1. Review previous day's input.

2. Some kinds of touch are against the rules. Give definitions.

- What is sexual abuse/assault?

- What types of touch are against the rules? When is someone emotionally, physically, or sexually hurt?

3. Differentiate touches that makes us feel good, warm, and safe from those that feel upsetting or confusing.

- Make a collage of pictures children cut out of examples of good-feeling and bad-feeling touch, or

- Give each child a touch match-up exercise (Activity Sheet #2) to complete and color.

- Emphasize hurtful touches could happen to anyone — old, young, boy, girl — and that anyone could break the rules.

4. Safety with strangers.

- Who is a stranger?

- Get options from children of what to do if they feel threatened, such as scream, run, stay in public areas, lock doors, trust feelings, say "no."

- Suggest and reinforce safety rules:

  ⤴ go with a buddy

  ⤴ ask permission to go anywhere, do anything

  ⤴ no secrets about touch

  ⤴ don't let anyone know if you are home alone

  ⤴ if lost in a store, stay and tell the clerk

  ⤴ make lots of noise if someone tries to take you or hurt you

5. Ask, "Who could break safety rules?"

  ⤴ emphasize it could be friends, family, grownups, babysitters, parents of a friend, older kids, kids the same age

6. Questions and answers

Optional:

1. Use posters. You could make these yourself to illustrate or purchase them.

2. Role plays.

3. Use hula hoops to show personal boundaries in different situations. Use two hula hoops, one for each person in the role play. Have the actors demonstrate how far their boundaries reach with a friend, a teacher, a stranger, someone who is mad at them? Have one push the boundary of the other back. What would the pushed person do? How would he or she feel?

Lesson 3: Options for Help

Objectives:

1. To present rules about prevention of sexual abuse or other safety issues.

2. To give options for what one can do/who one can tell.

3. To introduce assertive responses.

4. To reinforce concepts learned in the previous two days.

By end of presentation students will:

- State three prevention rules.

- Select personal and community resources for themselves.

- Demonstrate assertive behavior in role play situations and ways to say "no" to touch.

Materials needed: Blackboard, coloring sheets for each student or Support Tree; *No More Secrets* or *Who Do You Tell?* or other films, projector (optional)

Prerequisites: Lessons 1 and 2 (Three-Day Curriculum)

Length of Activity: 20-45 minutes

Age: 6-12

Size of Group: Maximum of 30

Suggested Groups: Elementary or developmentally disabled

Outline of Presentation: "Options for Help"

1. Brief review. Ask children what they've learned so far, and clarify any confusion.

2. Introduce three prevention skills. Relate to the rules discussed in Lesson 2.

   - Trust your feelings.

   - Be aware of your environment/make wise decisions.

   - Assert your boundaries. You have the right to say "no."

3. Use Options Chart.

- Ask children when it would be hardest to say "no" (with someone they know).

- Have them explore options if it's someone they know and like.

4. Practice saying "no." Give ideas for assertive communication.

- Role plays, use puppets, or

- Make a list on the blackboard of when they can say "no" to you or the teacher.

5. Show film *No More Secrets, Who Do You Tell?* or another film and discuss.

6. Resources discussion

- Personal — people in their own lives

- Community — police, teachers, store clerks

7. Coloring sheet or Support Tree to do at school or at home.

Optional:

1. Post-test.

2. Use posters.

3. Role plays.

4. Pass out crisis hotline cards to older students (grades 4-6).

5. End with another cooperative game.

Optional Activities

Trust Games

These can be used when discussing who a stranger is, and when and whom one can trust.

☑ Pair off students with a friend. One student closes his or her eyes while the other guides them around the classroom or hall. Guidance should be given with words and by holding hands. Now pair each student up with another they don't know quite as well. What was different? How soon did they open their eyes (stop trusting)? What makes us trust or distrust?

☑ Have eight to 12 students stand in a tight circle, facing toward the center. One person is in the middle. The center person makes his or her body stiff as a board. He or she keeps feet in stationary position and falls out to the hands of the people in the circle, his or her arms should be crossed in from of his or her chest. The persons in the circle pass the stiffened body around and across the circle. Slowly the circle widens as trust builds. The person in the center may stop the activity whenever he or she feels unsafe or uncomfortable. Of course, even saying "no" to doing this exercise should be applauded as an example of assertiveness.

Reporting Skills

Children need help in learning to remember details in case they ever need to report a suspicious car, person, or event. Two ways to practice are:

☑ Tell a story of a situation with a thief, molester, or "peeping tom" using a picture from a magazine that shows a crowd. Then put the picture down and ask the class to tell you everything they remember about the offender (age, size, clothes, location, car make and model).

☑ Stress that it's important to remember as much as you can about any person who bothers you. While discussing this, have a person (janitor, other teacher, secretary, aide) walk in and out of the room briefly to leave a message with you. Now ask the class to describe exactly what he or she looked like, said, and did.

Cooperative Games

A number of books available in the past have presented the concept of cooperative game-playing that oftentimes required positive interaction, rather than competitive effort to "win" at the game. These games are helpful in demonstrating fun and safe touch that need not result in "losers" in order to have "winners." The games should be carefully explained and demonstrated to ensure a good experience for each of the children with these exercises. These are only examples of some of the cooperative games that could be used to demonstrate touches that make us feel good:

☑ **Stand Up**

Pair children into groups of two with matches being made based on similar size and height. If the children are latent-age and squeamish about touching the opposite sex, encourage boys to find boys, girls to find girls.

Make certain desks, tables or any obstacles are moved to make adquate room for movement. Each pair will need space to sit back to back. They they will interlock arms and be instructed to work together to stand up together. Let them discover ways to cooperate to make this happen. (Hint: They may discover that by leaning against one another's backs they can accomplish this easier and more quickly.)

☑ **People Knots**

Have children stand in a circle, shoulder to shoulder. Have them each stretch their hands out to the center and grab another hand with each of their hands. The only rule is that they cannot grab two hands of the same person (or the game would be over already!). The group will have created a "knot" that will need to be untangled through people stepping over arms, twisting around, and moving together. When fnished, you should have another circle, or maybe two!

☑ **Mirror Image**

Instruct the youth to get into pairs and ask them to face one another about an arm's length apart. Have one individual be the one to move their arms and face/head slowly and ask the other to act as a mirror image to the other. This works best when done slowly, having the "mirror" match movements as exactly as possible. Then have the pair switch roles. Finish by having the class discuss the experience, which role they enjoyed best, and how it felt to be "mirrored."

☑ **On My Knees Please**

Make a circle with as many students as are in the class. Then have them all turn sideways in one direction and bring the circle in tighter to be chest-to-back all around. Instruct students to place their hands on the shoulder of the person in front of them. Then practice going to a sitting position to make certain everyone is lined up to have knees behind them to sit upon. Finally ask the group to say, "Sit on my knees please," as they slowly sit on the knees of the person directly behind them. Once everyone is secure you can see if the students can take their hands off the shoulders of the person in front of them as they sit comfortably.

Expanding Children's Options for Responding

☑ **What if . . . ? Games**

Besides the Options Chart, the "What if . . . ?" game can be helpful. This can be played quickly and often to help emphasize many of the safety concepts. Examples:

- What would you do if you were home alone with the babysitter and she started choking?

- What would you do if someone was following you home from school?

- What would you do if you were home alone and a fire started?

- What would you do if you got lost at the fair?

- What would you do if a uniformed officer told you they were supposed to drive you home?

☑ **Saying "No"**

- Help children practice ways to say "no" to a request from someone. This could be a request to share a candy bar, to go somewhere, perhaps to do something which a parent would not approve of. Talk about polite ways to communicate, forceful ways, and standing firm with one's own decision. When, if ever, is it OK to talk to a stranger? When is it OK when with your parents or another grownup in charge?

- We all have a right to say "no" sometimes. When? It's not our fault if that hurts the other person's feelings. We need to also respect our own feelings.

- Contrast assertive, aggressive, and passive ways to say "no." Saying, "It's against the rule," or "Mom won't let me," helps to put power on the child's side.

- Discuss verbal and nonverbal messages which help reinforce a "no." Do I look at the person while saying "no?" What does my body stance say? Am I laughing or serious? Do I move away? Does my tone of voice show I mean it?

Art Activities

☑ **Puppets**

Sock puppets, paper bag puppets, or more elaborate puppets can be used to act out role plays or "What if . . . ?" options. Shadow puppets are another fun approach. For shadow puppets, help children make animal or people shapes out of cardboard. Tape the shape to a stick or pencil so it can be held up. Next put up a sheet as a screen. Have children stand behind the sheet with a light behind them. They can kneel behind a table and hold up puppets which will case a shadow on the screen for the class to watch.

☑ **Warm Fuzzies and Cold Pricklies**

- Warm Fuzzies can be made out of yarn. Have children wrap yarn around a 2- by 3-inch piece of cardboard (around the 2-inch side). After getting to desired size, slip off mold and tie a string or rubber band tightly in the center. Then snip the loops and fluff. This will take some time, particularly if you try it with younger elementary students.

- Cold Pricklies need not be an art project, but you may wish to use them to illustrate the reading of "The Warm Fuzzy Story." Buy several small styrofoam balls and stick toothpicks all around. Be careful how you hold them!

Give each child a sturdy piece of paper, 8-1/2 by 11 inches, preferably poster board. Have the children each attach a string on two corners of the paper to make a loop large enough to comfortably fit over their necks and down their backs. Make available crayons, pens, pencils or markers for each child to write a "warm fuzzy" (something positive) message on the papers of six or more other children. Make sure it's set up so each child feels liked and accepted, not frustrated or rejected.

☑ **Touch Lines**

To stress the individual experience of touch, have each student take out a paper and make their own "touch lines." Those who write can personalize the touch line by identifying and writing down both the type of touch, from whom, and when they feel good, bad, or confused by the touch. For example:

MY TOUCH LINE

Good ☺*	Confusing ☺	Bad ☹
hug from Grandma at bedtime	slap from a friend when playing	hit from a big kid on the playground
kiss from Dad after school	tickled from neighbor when I say "no"	elbow from Mom in church

---

*For those who don't read, symbols and pictures can be used. Adults can then print the touch examples under the symbols or the children can draw the corresponding pictures of touches that made them feel happy, sad, or confused.

Language Arts Skills

☑ Word Bank — Make a list of new words related to this subject (crime, touch, victim, etc.) and write them on the board or make reversible cards with a word on one side and a definition or related picture on the other. These can be used for spelling words or vocabulary building.

☑ A list of word gifts that make us feel good, as does good touch, could be made (respectful, sharing, cheerful). These could be hung on a bulletin board and related to how we do or do not touch when we feel these ways.

Role Plays*

Two prime components critical to successful sexual abuse prevention are information and skills. Information may be transmitted in many ways, but skills are learned primarily through practice. The use of role plays and other theater techniques give children a safe and effective opportunity to learn and exercise preventive skills.

A teacher or youth worker desiring to give children this opportunity to improve prevention skills does not need to be skilled or experienced in acting or theater. Given a safe, open environment and enough information, most children respond quickly and enthusiastically to a chance to pretend. The objective of this activity is not to coach the children into polished performances, but simply to give them an opportunity to experiment and practice.

The following steps will help you encourage the participation of children:

☑ Use only volunteers for role plays. Do not draft students. Sexual abuse may be a current concern for some of the children.

☑ Do not comment on a child's performance as an actor. Evaluation should only concern the child's use of information and skills.

☑ A "creative" atmosphere needs to be established. A creative atmosphere is a balance between structure and freedom. Too much freedom leads to pandemonium. Too much structure stifles experimentation. Each leader will need to plan for and adjust to the needs of the specific group which she or he is leading.

The following are some possibilities for encouraging structure and freedom:

Structure

- An agreement to raise hands and speak one at a time.

- Recognition that personal safety is serious business.

- A list of questions to be answered (perhaps on the blackboard) and guidance from the leader when discussion strays from the questions.

- Strict silence and attention from the audience when actors role play.

- Desks clear of any unnecessary paper, pencils, or projects.

- The room should be arranged so that everyone can see clearly, but there should be a clear understanding when children may move and when they must sit.

---

*Developed by Don Yost and Carol Plummer, Bridgework Theater, Goshen, IN.

- There can be a discussion about laughing or making fun of someone who is acting or answering questions. A leader should be sensitive to the difference between nervous or supporting kinds of laughter and laughter that hurts or stifles a child.

Freedom

- A leader's own attitude is usually the key to freeing up the atmosphere. A willingness to listen and pay attention to every idea, no matter how silly it may sound at first is important. It says, "We are here to try things out, not to enforce or establish hard and fast rules."

- Trust is crucial to freedom and is a by-product of structure. Children should trust that they will not be harassed or belittled for any reason by classmates or, most importantly, by you, the leader.

- You will have some ideas of the right and wrong answers. Children will need at some point to have firm ideas of the safe and the unsafe things to do in any given situation, however, labeling answers or actions in a play as "right" or "wrong" can inhibit a child's willingness to venture guesses. A good technique for dealing with a "wrong" answer is to ask a question in return.

  Example:

  Leader: *What should Brenda do when her uncle tries to touch her?*
  Child: *Sock him in the mouth.*
  Leader: *Have you ever socked an adult in the mouth? What might happen?*

- Provide lots of positive reinforcement. Acting and answering can be frightening and children may need lots of encouragement and reassurance that they are doing fine.

- Freedom to follow a line of questioning or discussion for which you may not be prepared, but which seems important to the children.

- Answer and explain in a straightforward manner and to the best of your ability. If it is your opinion, let them know. If you don't know the answer, tell them that you will find out and be sure to report back.

☑ Role play is a specific theater technique, differing from theater in that the purpose has little to do with a performance or end product. Role play is valuable for the experience itself. People can experience emotions and situations unfamiliar to their own lives. Role play is not, however, improvisation, which at its extreme offers neither scripts, characters, nor settings. With role play, participants are usually assigned a character, history, and a setting. A participant in role play may also be given a script, or an outline of what to say. Many times creation of a dialogue is left up to the participants.

☑ In the suggested role plays, children are given a situation and a character. They are not given a script, but there are usually some suggestions of what to talk about and where the action should lead. Sometimes if a child seems "stuck," you can whisper a suggestion in their ears or ask children in the audience to share an idea.

70

Role Play 1: "Telling"

Reminder: Use only volunteers for role plays. Do not draft students (sexual abuse may be a current concern for some of the children).

Ages: 8-12

Objective: Give children practice in telling about sexual assault. Increase awareness that the story may have to be told several times.

Procedure:

1. Read background story.

    "Brenda has an uncle named John. She really likes him but lately Uncle John has been acting different. Sometimes he stares at her. He tells her dirty stories and tries to rub her between her legs."

2. Ask the students to list people whom Brenda (teacher, parent, aunt) could tell. Ask four students to play some of these people. Try to include two adult characters and two children (sibling, friend, cousin). Assign a character to each of the four students. Instruct two of them to be helpful to Brenda, and two be either too embarrassed or afraid to help her, or perhaps not even believe her. Try to give these instructions in writing or out of the earshot of the rest of the class.

3. Ask someone to play Brenda. Ask her to try to tell these people about her Uncle John. After she has attempted to tell, you may ask the class to suggest what Brenda should do next. It's encouraging to arrange it so that the last person Brenda tells is the most helpful. The main point is for children to keep telling until they find someone who is able and willing to help. Child confidantes should be encouraged to suggest the victim tell an adult and offer to go with them when they tell.

Role Play 2: "Good Touches"

Ages: 5-12

Objective: To demonstrate the need for good touches and the variety of touches people enjoy.

Procedure:

1. Ask the children to think of good touches they like to give to older persons, such as grandparents.

2. Have the teacher pretend to be the grandparent and sit in a chair at the front.

3. Choose volunteer students to come and give the "grandparent" (or whomever the child tells you the teacher should portray) a good touch.

4. Let as many children as possible take a turn.*

---

*Note: For older children, a mime of the touch may be more of a challenge and less embarrassing for them. Have the children in the audience guess the type of good touch being mimed.

Role Play 3: "Awareness"

Ages: 6-12

Objective: To increase awareness of types of touch. To give children practice in categorizing types of touch and in defining sexual abuse.

Procedure:

1. After the class has talked about different types of touch and the touch continuum, place a large chair in the front of the room. Ask different students to come up to the chair in the front and touch it in different ways (hug, kiss, kick, or ticklc).

2. The rest of the class may try to name or guess the kind of touch that is being mimed. List the different touches on the board.

3. Ask students whcther they would like to trade places with the chair if someone they liked touched them in that way. What if a stranger did?

4. Ask individual students where on the touch continuum he or she would place the touch and if he or she would need to tell anyone else about the touch.

Role Play 4: "Prevention"

Ages: 10-12

Objective: To increase awareness of different ways to prevent sexual abuse.

Procedure:

1. Set up two chairs at the front of the room. Tell the class that whoever sits in the one chair will pretend that they are trying to trick someone into touch that is wrong. Whoever sits in the second chair will pretend to be the person that could be tricked or trapped into sexual contact. If you feel that your students will have a hard time with the offender role, you as the teacher or an aide should play the role of the offender.

2. The two people in the chairs are to make up a story. The rest of the class will act as referees.

    The story is made up of "What if . . . ?" statements made by the offender. Example:

    Offender: *What if I followed you home from school?*

    Child: *I'd run as fast as I could.*

    Offender: *What if I ran faster than you?*

    Child: *I'd scream and yell like crazy.*

    Offender: *What if nobody heard you?*

3. Help the class keep in mind the purpose of this role play is not to "win." The object is to explore realistic alternatives to possible situations. This discourages the use of machine guns, karate, and other unrealistic tactics.

4. The rest of the class can help you by acting as referees. They may interrupt at points where they feel either are being unrealistic or if gets stuck. If someone is not able to respond, the class may discuss the choices which led to getting stuck.

5. Emphasize that if a child can't find a way out, it is still not his or her fault. Sometimes we all get stuck.

6. This is a verbal exchange. No touch should occur in this role play.

Role Play 5: "Support"

Ages: 9-12

Objective: To practice and increase awareness of peer support for persons victimized by sexual assault.

Procedure:

1. Read background story.

    "Alan was the oldest of three children. His parents were away at the movies one night and his two younger sisters were in bed. Because he was older, he was allowed to stay up an extra half-hour. He was sitting on the couch when the babysitter asked him if he liked girls.

    "Alan didn't know what to say. He liked his sisters and his mom but knew the babysitter meant something else. The babysitter asked him if he had ever seen a naked lady. She turned off the T.V. and pulled some Playboy pictures out of her books. Then she took off her clothes.

    "Finally she let Alan go to bed. He felt sick and embarrassed. He couldn't go to sleep. He decided that tomorrow he would tell his best friends, Tony and Bill, about it. Maybe they would know what to do."

2. Ask three boys to play Alan, Tony, and Bill. (If there are boys in your class with those names, be sure to substitute other names). Place three chairs in the front of the room. Tell Tony that he is to be as helpful as he can. Tell Bill that he will pretend to be unhelpful.

3. After the trio has tried some dialogue, ask the class to make suggestions about what would help Alan and statements that may make it worse. (Helpful — believe him, be serious, assist him in telling a trusted adult. Unhelpful — laugh, tell everyone else at school, call him a queer since he didn't feel comfortable, tell him he should have "gone for it," be real embarrassed.)

Guidelines for Introducing the Topic

Introducing a new topic can best be done by relating it to subjects already discussed in class. This could range from safety rules, to what crime in general is, to the fact that we have many senses, one of which is tactile — our sense of touch.

The main key in presenting information about preventing sexual abuse is to be comfortable with the subject and the curriculum material as a teacher. We have found these guidelines to be helpful in making us more comfortable as we discuss this sensitive topic.

For the Presenter

Make yourself comfortable . . . don't be embarrassed. You are sharing a safety concern similar to what to do if robbed, or if a fire or earthquake occurs.

- Use proper names of body parts. Slang or vague references may communicate to children that we are uncomfortable discussing this issue.

- Be clear, but somewhat general. Don't say, "It could be your father," but suggest that the offender could be a stranger, someone you know, or someone very close to you.

- Note facial, body, and verbal responses. Deal with their embarrassment first.

- Respect the child's pace of learning. Repeat as needed.

Information to Be Shared with Children

- Touch can make you feel good or bad. Give examples and ask for their examples.

- Some touch is confusing or doesn't feel good.

- Trust your feelings/intuitions.

- You have the right to tell a person "no" if he touches you or asks you to touch him.

- You have the right to talk to a trusted adult if someone touches you in a confusing or hurtful manner — or whenever you feel upset or uncomfortable with anything.

- It is not your fault if someone touches or hurts you, even if you made unwise decisions that helped to trap you.

- Secrets are not OK unless they are about something positive, like a birthday surprise.

- People can get into difficult situations, but that doesn't mean they are "bad people."

- Adults and older kids who improperly touch or hurt you have a problem and need help. It's important to tell, so they can get help.

Pre- and Post-Test for Elementary Students

I am a ☐ boy ☐ girl

I am in grade _____.

1. Most touches are good.

   ☐ Yes ☐ No

2. Sometimes it's good to tell secrets.

   ☐ Yes ☐ No

3. Sometimes relatives touch children in ways that confuse them.

   ☐ Yes ☐ No

4. If someone touched my private parts it would be because I wasn't careful enough.

   ☐ Yes ☐ No

5. Sexual abuse is the same as getting beat up.

   ☐ Yes ☐ No

6. If a friend tells you he was hurt by a grownup, he is probably telling the truth.

   ☐ Yes ☐ No

7. Bad touches are touches that make you feel bad inside.

   ☐ Yes ☐ No

8. If someone touches your private parts and says not to tell anyone, *that* is sexual abuse.

   ☐ Yes ☐ No

9. If your friend told you somebody touched him and he didn't like it, go with him to tell a grownup.

   ☐ Yes ☐ No

10. Could someone who hurts a child be someone she knows?

    ☐ Yes ☐ No

11. The only people who can help you if you have a problem are your relatives.

    ☐ Yes ☐ No

12. If the first grownup you tell about a problem doesn't help you, you should forget about the problem.

   ❏ Yes   ❏ No

13. The only thing you can do if a grownup touches you in ways you don't like is to stay away from them.

   ❏ Yes   ❏ No

14. The best way to protect yourself from a bad touch is to hit the person who touches you.

   ❏ Yes   ❏ No

15. If another person touches you in ways you don't like, is it partly your fault?

   ❏ Yes   ❏ No

16. It's a good idea to yell if someone touches you in a way that scares you.

   ❏ Yes   ❏ No

17. If you have a problem, keep telling grownups until you get help.

   ❏ Yes   ❏ No

Pre- and Post-Test Answers for Elementary Students

1.	Yes	10.	Yes
2.	Yes	11.	No
3.	Yes	12.	No
4.	No	13.	No
5.	No	14.	No
6.	Yes	15.	No
7.	Yes	16.	Yes
8.	Yes	17.	Yes
9.	Yes		

Sample Letters to Parents

Some schools or teachers may want to use letters similar to the ones below to inform parents about sexual abuse prevention programs. Many times the issue has just been incorporated into safety classes. Focusing special attention upon informing parents has the potential for making parents feel it must be a matter of alarm or controversy.

The first letter would be used before the program was introduced. A permission slip might be added to the bottom of the letter if desired.

The second letter would be sent home with students following the presentation(s).

Letter #1

Dear Parents,

We are starting a new unit in your child's class at school and want to make you aware of it so you can answer his or her questions and continue our classroom discussions at home.

In the past few years we all have become increasingly concerned with the safety of our children. Unfortunately, each year over 100,000 young people are sexually assaulted in our country. Often the children are as young as seven or eight.

We are planning a unit to talk with children about this safety concern. We will be discussing types of good and bad touch, and stress the importance of talking to a trusted adult whenever he or she feels confused or doesn't like a touch from someone. We'll be discussing things children can do prevent harm and also teaching some assertive skills, such as you have the right to say "no" to touch you dislike.

Feel free to call me if you have further questions.

OR

A PTO meeting to talk about this program is scheduled for _____.
Please plan to attend and help us work on this problem together.

Sincerely,

The follow-up letter should include this information:

Letter #2

Dear Parents,

Your child has just learned about an important safety issue — the prevention of child sexual abuse. Because you are the most important teacher to your child, we want to share the important aspects of this program so that you can further discuss this issue at home.

Points to Stress

1. Touch can be good, bad, or confusing.

2. Pay attention to your feelings if you feel uncomfortable about a touch.

3. If you don't like a touch or feel confused by it, talk to a grownup whom you trust.

4. It's OK to say "no" if someone confuses or embarrasses you with a touch, or, if someone touches your "private parts."

hug

5. Anyone could be a sexual abuse victim (the person who is harmed). Anyone could be an offender (the person who hurts the victim).

6. Always tell a trusted adult if you are touched in ways that feel bad or confusing, even if you were told it was a secret. Keep telling if you don't get help.

7. It's never your fault if you get touched in these ways (are sexually abused).

Some Safety Rules Your Child Learned

1. Do not go anywhere alone or with others without permission from the adult in charge (parent, teacher, babysitter).

Letter #2 continued on next page

---

2.   Do not talk to strangers unless you are with your parents or another trusted adult.

3.   Go places with a buddy.

4.   Always tell a grownup if someone makes you feel uncomfortable or tries to hurt you.

5.   It's OK to say "no" to touch you don't like.

6.   Don't keep secrets about touches that hurt your body or your feelings.

Exercises

Some ways to find out what your child understands include:

1.   Ask your child to describe the type(s) of touch pictured on this and the previous page. "When could this touch be confusing? Or bad? Good? What should you do if touch feels uncomfortable or if you are unsure whether it is really 'bad'?"

2.   Ask your child: "Who are some people you could talk with if you had any kind of problem?"

3.   Play the "What if . . . ?" game frequently with your child. Ask your child: "What would you do?" in any of a number of potentially dangerous situations. For example: "What if . . . you got lost in a department store?"

"What if . . . someone was following you on the way home from school and you felt frightened?"

"What if . . . you saw a fire at the neighbor's house?"

"What if . . . your club leader started touching you in ways you didn't like?"

Add other questions about situations that could happen in your child's daily life.

Letter #2 continued on next page

4. Keep this paper for reference so you can repeat this process again in several months.

Remember

- Over 100,000 children are sexually abused in the U.S. every year.

- Most are abused by people they know rather than strangers.

- Both boys and girls are victims.

- Sexual abuse spans all income, ethnic, and religious groups.

- And, we adults should do everything possible to stop and prevent this problem. If you know of a child who is being abused in any way, help them by calling your local child protective services agency at _____.

Keep in mind that your report and identity will remain confidential.

If you have any questions about this letter or our program, please do not hesitate to call me.

Sincerely,

"The Warm Fuzzy Story"
A Modern Folktale

Once upon a time, a long, long time ago, there was a place called Warm Fuzzy Land. Everyone who was born in Warm Fuzzy Land received a bag of Warm Fuzzies. Everyone who lived there was very happy and contented. This was because they gave and received Warm Fuzzies. A Warm Fuzzy is a soft ball that seems to melt right into you when you receive it. It gives you a nice warm, happy, loving feeling. They heard from the old folks that one could never, ever run out of Warm Fuzzies. They would have Warm Fuzzies forever to give to each other.

Then one day a stranger came to town. He talked with some of the people and told them that he was sure they had been lied to; eventually they would run out of Warm Fuzzies. There was not, after all, an unlimited supply of anything. He sounded rather smart. This idea frightened the people and they began to be "careful" with their Warm Fuzzies and, eventually downright selfish. They only gave them out on special occasions, like birthdays, Christmas, and other holidays. Their friends also got stingy. Since people didn't want to give out Warm Fuzzies, they never received them.

Well, Warm Fuzzy Land changed a lot. People weren't as warm or friendly anymore. People even avoided each other so they wouldn't have to share Warm Fuzzies. The place was getting so unhappy that some people were actually getting very sick from never getting any Warm Fuzzies.

Then a doctor-of-sorts came into town, with a cure for everything. He was stumped at first but created a replacement for Warm Fuzzies. He called them Cold Pricklies. This way people could exchange something when they met and it kept people from getting so sick. But they looked and felt, cold, prickly, and nobody liked them much.

After a while someone got the idea of making a Fake Fuzzy. Fake Fuzzies looked like Warm Fuzzies on the outside but inside they were really Cold Pricklies. People expecting to get a Warm Fuzzy ended by being tricked because they actually were cold and prickly inside.

With the spring, someone new came to town. She was called the Hip Woman. She gave out Warm Fuzzies to everyone, just like in the old days. She didn't believe she'd ever run out. The children all fell in love with the Hip Woman since she was so nice and freely gave to them. Soon they too believed they'd never run out and gave Warm Fuzzies to everyone. Once again the children were happy.

The parents were worried by the recklessness of their children and passed laws saying Warm Fuzzies could only be exchanged on special occasions. But the children kept on passing out Warm Fuzzies and being happy. Eventually, the grownups decided they wanted to be happy again, like in the old days. They tried giving out Warm Fuzzies and they didn't run out! Everyone was smiling and happy again. They burned all the Cold Pricklies and Fake Fuzzies and lived happily ever after.

The End

Who can you talk to when you feel confused or bothered ?

85

How do these touches feel ?

:) good   ? confusing   :(bad

hug

kick

Kiss

punch

holding hands

piggy-back ride

push

squeeze

© 1979 The Illusion Theater, Inc

The Support Tree

Clubs

1. _____
2. _____
3. _____

Sports

1. _____
2. _____
3. _____

School

1. _____
2. _____
3. _____

Religious or Church

1. _____
2. _____
3. _____

Family

1. _____
2. _____
3. _____

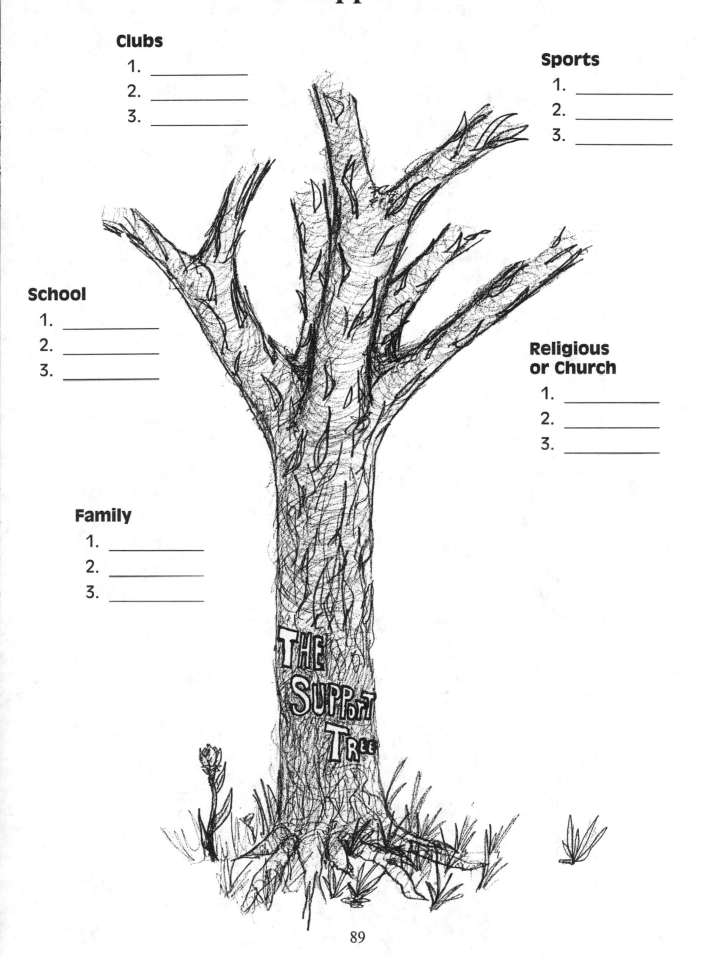

7
Curriculum and Lesson Plans: For Grades 7-12

7
Curriculum and Lesson Plans:
For Grades 7-12

Basic Concepts to Communicate to Students

1. Sexual abuse threatens our safety; it is a serious problem nationally as well as locally.

2. Sexual abuse includes abuse from a stranger, incest, and acquaintance rape.

3. Sexual abuse includes being tricked, manipulated, or forced into sexual contact.

4. Forced or tricked sexual contact can be "hands-on" such as rape, molestation or "hands-off" abuse such as obscene phone calls, or witnessing someone expose him or herself.

5. Sexual abuse can sometimes be prevented by:

   ■ trusting our feelings of danger or discomfort;

   ■ remaining aware of our environment and situations we are getting into,

   ■ and asserting our personal boundaries.

6. The victim of sexual abuse is never to blame for that abuse.

7. If abuse occurs, tell trusted friends or adults until someone believes you and helps you.

8. Support and assistance is important to give to friends who have been victimized. This support could also be important for children as we become parents ourselves.

Using the Curriculum and Lesson Plans

On page 96 you will find an overview for a five-day presentation, on page 97 is the overview for three-day presentation, and a one-day presentation overview on page 98. Choose a program based upon your group's needs and your time constraints. The numbers you will see in parentheses in the overview refer you to pages where further guidelines on the use of that activity are provided. After choosing a one-, three-, or five-day presentation, turn to the appropriate pages that follow for daily lesson plans. Look over the objectives, materials needed, and the lesson outline. Which activities would your students most enjoy? Which activities would have the greatest potential for learning new skills? How much time can you spend with this material? Transfer some activities, if desired, from one day to another, or from the three-day to the five-day program. Add other activities from the "Optional Activities" section. Good luck. Be prepared for surprises. You will probably learn as much as your students and you may find these sessions to be as enjoyable as they are important.

This section of the book gives an outline for presentations to students from grades seven through 12. Because of the wide age range and ability level variations in maturity levels, teachers will need to choose activities and time segments most appropriate to their groups of students. Some of our findings, made through trial and error, may help you in making those determinations.

Through involvement with our project and contacts with other professionals we are convinced that adolescents can be empowered to help prevent their own victimization. But first they must be told clearly what sexual abuse is, ways it may happen, and helped to distinguish abuse from sexuality.

Distinguishing healthy sexual interest or activity from abuse is not an easy task. Indeed, adults may confuse the two since the line between them on the "touch continuum" is a fuzzy one. We all want and need some form of attention, affection, and touch. Yet, each of us also needs to feel in control of our own interactions, our own bodies, and our own lives. We all have and need boundaries.

For adolescents, this confusion is compounded. Unlike younger children, there is more interest in sexuality as their bodies and minds mature. Yet, they are inexperienced. Fantasies of love are interwoven by advertising which glamorizes early sexual involvement rather than by real-life advice from parents or other responsible adults. Even more unfortunate is the type of sex that is glamorized: objectification of partners, the "catching" or "conquering" of a partner, force and violence as an expression of love, ownership of one person by another — often depicted as healthy human sexual expression.

Prevention programs should neither advocate nor condemn sexual involvement by teenagers. However, the fact remains that it exists. It is estimated that at least 12 million teens were sexually active in the United States in 1982. Under the age of 14, 18 percent of all boys and 6 percent of all girls have had intercourse. In addition, sex and sexual abuse are nearly indistinguishable for teens, except in the most extreme cases. Several recently published studies have also shown us that approximately half of teen mothers were sexual abuse victims and a large number were impregnated by men 10 or more years older than themselves! This program attempts to help correct that — to help teens draw clearer lines, to condemn sexual abuse for the trap that it is, and to empower youth with a new clarity, a new certainty needed to maintain their personal safety.

Tips for Working with Grades 7-9

☑ Most of the activities in the curriculum are suited for this age group. Use your discretion based on knowledge of your particular audience. The most unsuitable activities are designated.

☑ With this age group there may be some discomfort or inappropriate laughter about this topic. Acknowledging the laughter as embarrassment, telling them you are convinced they are mature enough to talk about this serious problem, and sharing some statistics goes a long way toward resolving this nervousness.

Victim-blaming will be common in this age group. Use some of the activities which address this issue directly. It can be frustrating, but is an important issue. This may also be related to sex role stereotypes which this age group has preoccupations with at this stage of their identity development.

Early adolescence is when many victims, particularly incest victims, first disclose sexual abuse. They may tell directly about long-term abuse as they recognize it is not "normal," and as increased independence strengthens them to feel they did not have to put up with it. They may also tell indirectly by abusing drugs, running away from home, promiscuity, or talking to you about "a friend of mine who has this problem."

Tips for Working with Grades 10-12

It is most often useful to tie this curriculum directly into the subject usually taught during this class period. When the focus, however, is "Child Development" or "Family Living" or "Sociology" the tendency may be to intellectualize the problem too much and get bogged down in statistics. As a leader, be certain to make the issue real to the students. It has certainly touched the lives of some in your group and will touch the lives of more. The primary aim should still be on gaining applicable skills to help them prevent sexual victimization of themselves and others, rather than a memorization of facts about "that problem out there."

Be especially aware that, in a group of young adults, you may be speaking to any or all of the following:

- past, present, or future victims

- past, present, or future offenders

- present or future parents

Remembering that helps us to recognize the importance of addressing this population despite the tendency for the focus of such prevention programs to be entirely upon elementary level youngsters. There should be special focus on the community resources available to help those hurt by the problem of sexual abuse — victims, offenders, and family members.

Five-Day Curriculum Overview

Day 1: The Problem	Day 2: Strangers	Day 3: Incest	Day 4: Acquaintance Rape and Sexual Harassment	Day 5: Prevention and Resources
1. Introduce topic with select facts (151)*	1. Ask class to define "strangers"	1. Select and read incest case studies (145)	1. Give definitions (153)	1. Discuss: Are there ways to prevent abuse?
2. Relate presentation to subject studied in class (141)	2. Dispel myths about places and persons who abuse (151)	2. Explain confusion of boundaries (161)	2. When is it rape/assault? • Ask students' views	2. Prevention skills (159) • Trust your feelings • Be aware of environment • Assert boundaries
3. Explain touch continuum on board (155) and do role plays	3. Use Options Chart (157) to show examples of relating to strangers	3. Divide class into four groups for discussion • father/offender • daughter/victim • sibling • mother	3. Discuss sexual peer pressure • Hula hoops (117) • Set boundaries before dates • Communicating limits during dates	3. Assertive behaviors • Definition • Contrast passive, assertive, aggressive behaviors
4. Give definitions (153)	4. List typical "stranger" warnings	4. Spokesperson summarizes group discussions	4. Role Play 1 (122)	4. Resources (160) • Personal • Community
5. Role Play 6 (127)	5. Introduce: offenders can be family, acquaintances, or friends • Harder to handle • Power dynamics	5. Role Play 2 (123)	5. Are victims to blame? What kinds of persons are abused? • Victim's Panel (137) • Optional Activities (117)	5. Role Play 4 (125)
6. Discussion. Questions and answers.	6. Do Role Play 5 (126)	6. Supporting friends • Show supportive and non-supportive responses • Role Play 3 (124)		6. Discussion. Questions and answers.
	7. Discussion. Questions and answers.	7. Discussion. Questions and answers.		

Optional:	Optional:	Optional:	Optional:	Optional:
1. Pre-test (131) 2. Do values line exercise (117)	1. Outline profiles of offenders • Fixated • Regressed 2. Use the *Acquaintance Rape* film about a stranger met at a party, *The Party Game* (171)	1. Show part of *Out of the Trap* or other film or video showing problems associated with incest (172)	1. Show film 2. Spend more time and use entire *Acquaintance Rape* series or another series of videotapes or films (171)	1. Case study analysis 2. Post-test (131) or values line (117) 3. Hand out crisis hotline cards 4. Guest speaker

*( ) Indicates cross reference to related page number.

Three-Day Curriculum Overview

We recommend at least three days to adequately cover the topic. However, when time does not allow, some information is preferable to none so we have included a one-day presentation option on the following page.

Day 1: Problem Overview

1. Introduce topic with fact sheet (151)*
2. Ask for and then clarify definitions (153)
3. Relate topic to class subject taught (141)
4. Explain touch continuum on board (155)
5. Use role play suggestions from class on types of touch
6. Read and discuss select case studies (145)
7. Choose one or two role play options (120)
8. Discussion. Questions and answers.

Optional:

1. Do pre-test (131)
2. Prepare bulletin board with posters, news clippings, etc.

Day 2: Focus on Incest

1. Read and discuss incest case studies (145)
2. Discuss incest indicators using sheet (161)
   - Boundaries
   - Crisis period
   - High-risk groups
   - Fears of disclosure
3. Choose one or two role play options (120)
4. List reasons to report or not to report from class suggestions
5. Use Options Chart (157)
6. Discussion. Questions and answers.

Optional:

1. Use previous or subsequent class to view a videotape or film play about incest (171)

Day 3: Focus on Prevention Skills

1. Define acquaintance rape/sexual harassment (153). Discuss:
   - Why is it easy to feel trapped?
   - Why is it easy to blame self?
2. Present prevention skills (159)
   - Trust your feelings
   - Be aware of your environment
   - Assert your boundaries
3. Define and role play aggressive, assertive, passive behaviors
4. Discuss laws and penalties
5. Resources (160)
   - Personal
   - Community

Optional:

1. Have students do a case study analysis to test learning
2. Give post-test (131)
3. Follow up with a series of films on the topic

---

*( ) Indicates cross reference to related page number.

One-Day Curriculum

Day 1: Presentation

---

1. Introduce topic with select facts (151)

2. Give definitions (153)

3. Explain touch continuum on the board (155)

4. Read and discuss two to four case studies (145)

5. Discussion: The victim is never to blame (118)

6. Prevention skills (159)

    - Trust your feelings
    - Be aware of your environment
    - Assert your boundaries

7. Resources (160)

    - Personal
    - Community

Optional:

---

1. Hand out crisis hotline cards.

2. Relate to the subject taught in an ongoing way (141)

3. Do a more complete input/review later in the school year

---

*( ) indicates cross reference to related page number.

Lesson 1: The Problem

Objectives:

1. To determine the attitudes and facts students perceive regarding child sexual abuse.

2. To introduce the touch continuum and definitions.

3. To integrate the topic with the class subject being taught.

By end of presentation students will:

- Discuss the problem as one form of child abuse

- List types of touch from the touch continuum.

- Compare sexual abuse with other forms of child abuse.

Materials needed: Blackboard, Pre-test (optional)

Length of activity: 45–60 minutes

Age: 12–18

Size of group: Maximum of 40

Suggested group: Middle and High School

Outline of Presentation: "The Problem"

1. Introduce the topic with selected facts from fact sheet.

2. Relate the presentation to the subject being studied in class. Pick one topic from Notes to Teachers to discuss as the opener.

3. Put Touch Continuum on the board to explain types of touch. Have students role play types of good, bad, and confusing touches.

4. Ask for, then clarify definitions.

5. Do Role Play 6.

6. Discussion. Questions and answers.

Optional:

1. Pre-test.

2. Values Line.

Lesson 2: Strangers

Objectives:

1. To focus the class on abuse by strangers, types of offenders, ways children get tricked or trapped.

2. To introduce prevention ideas and establish that not all offenders are strangers.

By end of presentation students will:

- Differentiate types of offenders' tricks, or traps.

- Explore options for responding to potential abuse.

- Role play confrontations with strangers/family friends.

Materials needed: Blackboard; Acquaintance Rape film, projector, and screen (optional)

Prerequisites: Lesson 1 (Five-Day Curriculum)

Age: 12-18

Size of group: Maximum of 40

Suggested group: Middle and High School

Outline of Presentation: "Strangers"

1. Have the class define "strangers."

2. Dispel myths about places and persons who abuse — for example, less than 25 percent of sexually abused children are strangers to the offender.

3. Use Options Chart to show examples of strangers as potential offenders.

4. List typical "stranger" warnings from students' examples.

5. Introduce: Offenders can be family, friends, or acquaintances.

   - Harder to handle when you know them.

   - Power dynamics. Do Role Play 5 with student volunteers.

6. Discussion. Questions and answers.

Optional:

1.   Outline profiles of offenders.

     •   Fixated — prefers relating to children. Treatment is difficult.

     •   Regressed — during a crisis period reverted back to sexual contact with children. May be easier to treat.

2.   Show film.

Lesson 3: Incest

Objectives:

1.   To isolate incest as one type of sexual abuse.

2.   To evaluate the family dynamics in incest.

3.   To classify options for victims to get out of the abuse environment.

By the end of presentation students will:

- Define incest.

- Detect situations that are high risk for incest.

- Select options a victim could attempt.

- State ways to support victimized friends.

Materials Needed: Blackboard; videotape and videotape player or film (optional)

Prerequisites: Lesson 1, 2 (Five-Day Curriculum)

Length of Activity: 45-60 minutes

Age: 12-18

Size of Group: Maximum of 40

Suggested Group: Middle or High School

Outline of Presentation: "Incest"

1.   Select and read several incest case studies.

2.   Explain confusion of boundaries.

3.   Divide the class into four groups to determine how each might feel in an incestuous family. Have each group discuss and list the range of feelings and options they think they would have.

- Father/Offender

- Daughter/Victim

- ■ Sibling

- ■ Mother

4. Have a spokesperson from each group summarize the small-group discussion for the whole class.

5. Role Play 2

6. Supporting friends

- ■ List on board suggestions for helpful and non-helpful responses.

- ■ Do Role Play 3 to practice skills.

7. Discussion. Questions and answers.

Optional:

Show segment of *Out of the Trap* videotape or other tape or film on this topic that explores problems associated with incest.

Lesson 4: Acquaintance Rape and Sexual Harassment

Objectives:

1. To define acquaintance rape/sexual harassment.

2. To give students information on state law.

3. To discuss pressure to have sexual contact with peers and teach students skills in setting boundaries and saying no.

By end of presentation students will:

■   Summarize the law about types of sexual abuse.

■   Describe acquaintance rape/sexual harassment.

■   Practice skills in refusing sexual contact.

Materials needed: Blackboard; films: *The Party Game* or *The Date*, projector, screen, hula hoops (optional)

Prerequisites: Lessons, 1, 2, 3 (Five-Day Curriculum)

Length of activity: 45-60 minutes

Age: 12-18

Size of group: Maximum of 40

Suggested Group: Middle or High School

Outline of Presentation: "Acquaintance Rape and Sexual Harassment"

1. Give definitions of acquaintance rape and sexual harassment.

2. Ask: When is it rape?

    ■   List students' attitudes and comments.

    ■   Read your state law.

    ■   Read the school's policy on sexual harassment.

3. Discussion: Pressures to be sexually involved with peers.

    ■   Use hula hoops to demonstrate your body is your own.

    ■   Encourage setting touch boundaries before dates.

    ■   How could one communicate during dates about limits to touch? Or to a boss about limits to jokes or sexual comments at work.

4. Do Role Play 1 to practice skills in refusing sexual advances.

5. Are victims ever to blame? What kinds of persons are abused?

    ■   Victim's Panel Exercise.

    ■   Optional Activities.

Optional:

1. Show an acquaintance/date rape film.

2. Spend more time and use series of videos or films about rape, sexual harassment, assertiveness, and dating safety.

Lesson 5: Prevention and Resources

Objectives:

1. To contrast aggressive, passive, and assertive behaviors.

2. To establish some prevention guidelines for students.

3. To specify personal and community resources for victims.

By end of presentation students will:

■   Rephrase definition of aggressive, passive, and assertive behaviors.

■   Trace local reporting procedures.

■   Choose personal and community resources to use if victimized.

■   Practice assertive skills.

Materials needed: Crisis hotline cards and post-test (optional)

Prerequisites: Lessons 1, 2, 3, 4 (Five-Day Curriculum)

Length of activity: 45-60 minutes

Age: 12-18

Size of group: Maximum of 40

Suggested group: Middle or High School

Outline of Presentation: "Prevention and Resources"

Open discussion topic:

1. Are there ways to prevent abuse and sexual harassment?

2. List Prevention Skills. Define all the terms and get examples in role plays or description of each.

    ■   Trust your feelings.

    ■   Be aware of your environment.

- Assert your boundaries.

3. Assertive behaviors

    - Give a clear definition.

    - Contrast an assertive response to the problem with an aggressive and a passive one in three role plays of the same situation. (Saying "no" to unwanted touch of some kind.)

4. Explore resources for reporting/helping.

    - Personal — friends, family

    - Community — school, clergy, therapist, or police.

5. Line up — Role Play 4.

6. Discussion. Questions and answers.

Optional:

1. Have students do a case study analysis to test learning.

2. Give post-test or do values line again.

3. Hand out crisis hotline cards as a community resource.

4. Having a guest speaker available to talk about local resources and programs is often of interest to students (for example, from child protective services, a sexual assault program, or a therapist who works with adult survivors).

Lesson 1: Problem Overview

Objectives:

1. To give facts about child sexual abuse, define sexual assault terms, and introduce touch continuum.

2. To integrate topic with class subject taught.

3. To summarize facts on offenders, victims, and ways victims get trapped.

By end of presentation students will:

■ Explain types of touch and sexual assault.

■ List ways victims get trapped by sexual abuse.

■ Identify common characteristics of offenders.

Materials needed: Blackboard, Pre-test (optional)

Prerequisites: None

Length of activity: 45-60 minutes

Age: 12-18

Size of group: Maximum of 40

Suggested group: Middle or High School

Outline of Presentation: "Problem Overview"

1. Introduce topic with facts. Use the fact sheet.

2. Ask for definitions of key terms, clarify and expand definition.

3. Relate to subject studied in class.

4. Explain touch continuum on the board. Use role plays from student suggestions of good, bad, and confusing touches. Emphasize no touch is inherently "good" or "bad," it is individually determined how the youth feels about the touch.

5. Read and discuss several case studies.

   ■ Identify characteristics and techniques offenders use.

     ◆ secrecy — "It's best if we keep this just between us. Others won't understand."

     ◆ bribes — giving money or gifts to buy cooperation or secrecy.

     ◆ drugs or alcohol — given to make a young person feel grown up, indebted, or incapacitated.

     ◆ blackmailed — "I'll have to show them the photos you let me take of you."

     ◆ "grooming" — where behavior starts "innocently" with a backrub or pat on the knee, but over time gradually escalates to more overt sexual touch.

     ◆ flattery — "You're so pretty I couldn't help myself." "You're so mature for your age."

   ■ Identify ways victims are trapped.

     ◆ Forced, tricked, or confused into cooperation.

     ◆ Trapped into not reporting or ending abuse.

6. Choose one or two role play options for students to demonstrate.

   ■ Help students put themselves in victim's place. Reinforce that victims can be male or female.

   ■ Help students empathize and support the victim (not blame).

7. Discussion. Questions and answers.

Optional:

1. Do pre-test.

2. Prepare bulletin board with posters and news clippings related to the topic of sexual assault or child sexual abuse.

Lesson 2: Focus on Incest

Objectives:

1. To isolate incest as one type of sexual abuse.

2. To evaluate the family dynamics of incest, including reasons to keep the family secret.

3. To classify options for victims to get out of the abusive environment.

By end of presentation students will:

- Differentiate incest from other types of child sexual abuse.

- Detect situations that are high risk for incest.

- Identify reasons not to report and reasons to report incest.

- Select options for victims.

Materials needed: Blackboard, hula hoops, an educational videotape and player (optional).

Prerequisites: Lesson 1 (Three-Day Curriculum)

Length of Activity: 45-60 minutes

Age: 12-18

Size of group: Maximum of 40

Suggested group: Middle or High School

Outline of Presentation: "Focus on Incest"

1. Choose several incest case studies, read and discuss.

2. Discuss incest indicators.

   - Demonstrate family boundaries using hula hoops. Hula hoops may be used to illustrate personal boundaries concept.

   - Crisis period.

   - High-risk group.

   - Fears of disclosure.

3.   Choose one or two role plays for students to act out.

■   Who and how to tell about incest.

■   Typical responses when one reports (anger, disbelief, blame of victim, fear, self-blame, or nervousness).

4.   Reasons to report or not report — make a list on the blackboard from students' suggestions.

5.   Use Options Chart to explore:

■   Ways to get out of a specific situation.

■   What might happen if one does/doesn't report.

6.   Discussion. Questions and answers.

Optional:

Use previous or subsequent class to view a videotape about sexual abuse or incest.

Lesson 3: Focus on Prevention Skills

Objectives:

1. To contrast aggressive, passive, and assertive behaviors.

2. To explain acquaintance rape and sexual harassment as two forms of sexual abuse.

3. To categorize laws regarding types of abuse and reporting guidelines.

4. To specify personal and local community resources for victims.

5. To list and explain several prevention guidelines.

By end of presentation students will:

■ Rephrase definitions of aggressive, passive, and assertive behaviors.

■ Describe acquaintance rape.

■ Define sexual harassment.

■ Summarize the state law about types of abuse and how to report.

■ Choose personal and community resources to use if they are victimized.

■ List and practice prevention skills.

Materials needed: Blackboard, crisis hotline cards, and post-test (optional).

Prerequisites: Lessons 1, 2 (Three-Day Curriculum)

Length of activity: 45-60 minutes

Age: 12-18

Size of group: Maximum of 40

Suggested group: Middle or High School

Outline of Presentation: "Focus on Prevention Skills"

1. Define acquaintance rape, date rape, and sexual harassment.

    ■ Discuss: Why is it easy to feel trapped?

- Discuss: Why is it easy to blame yourself?

2. Present prevention skills.

   - Trust your feelings.

   - Be aware of your environment.

   - Assert your boundaries.

3. Define and role play aggressive, assertive, and passive behaviors.

   - Give definitions

   - Role plays (same situation done all three ways). Role Play 7 works quite well.

4. Discuss laws and penalties. Sexual assault and sexual harassment are crimes.

   - Discuss: When is it abuse/rape/harassment?

   - Role play: To whom/when/where/how should it be reported?

5. Using resources when one needs help or support.

   - Personal — friends, family.

   - Community — school, clergy, crisis hotline, therapist, protective services, or police.

   - The resource we choose will be different for each of us. What's important is that we trust the resource and keep telling until we find help.

Optional:

1. Hand out crisis hotline cards.

2. Have students do a case study analysis to test their learning.

3. Give post-test.

4. Follow up with a film on related topics.

One-Day Presentation

Note: Due to limited time, only lecture-style teaching is suitable to cover this material.

Objectives:

1. To define sexual assault terms and familiarize students with the topic of child sexual abuse.

2. To emphasize prevention skills and personal and community resources if harassed or victimized.

By end of presentation student will:

- Discriminate types of sexual assault.
- Identify types of touch.
- List three prevention skills.
- Select usable personal and community resources.

Materials needed: Blackboard, crisis hotline cards (optional)

Prerequisites: None

Length of Activity: 45–60 minutes

Age: 12–18

Size of Group: Maximum of 40

Suggested Group: Middle or High School

Outline of Presentation:

1. Introduce topic with select facts.

2. Give definitions.

3. Explain touch continuum on the board.

4. Read and discuss two to four case studies.

5. Discussion: The victim is *never* to blame.

   ■ Stress the offender's responsibility.

   ■ No one asks to be forced or tricked into sex.

   ■ Would a male victim be blamed for what he wears or for being alone?

6. Prevention skills.

   ■ Trust your feelings.

   ■ Be aware of your environment.

   ■ Assert your boundaries.

7. Discuss personal and community resources

   ■ Adults and peers who students know and trust.

   ■ Crisis hotline, counseling centers, protective services, and police.

Optional:

1. Hand out crisis hotline cards.

2. Relate to the subject taught in an ongoing way

3. Do a more complete input/review later in the school year

Optional Activities

Saying "No" to Touch

☑ Have each student pretend to be a parent. Acting as parents, have students make lists of when their children could or could not say "no" to them. Share lists in small group discussions.

☑ Divide the class in half. Give one half a "valued object." (This could be a pencil, paper cup, penny, etc.) The owners are told (secretly) to do whatever they can to get possession of the object (bribe, trick, ask, etc.). Tell them not to use physical force but note how soon they feel like it. Discuss: How does it feel to say "no," or to be told "no"? How might offenders feel when rejected? Does such frustration, though real, justify hurtful or violent behavior?

☑ Hula hoops and boundaries — each of us owns our own body. We all feel we have a certain amount of space around us that belongs to us. Use two students with hula hoops to demonstrate their space boundaries. Tell them to adjust their boundaries as they speak to a boss, a disliked teacher, their father, a girl or boy friend. Abuse occurs when someone else doesn't respect their boundary, and crosses it, or forcibly changes it. Discuss how boundaries are different based on family, culture, personality, etc.

Images of Males/Females/Children

☑ Discuss: Is abuse of women related to abuse of children? How is it the same? Different?

☑ Have students bring in pictures of adults made to look or act like children in advertisements. Also, bring a magazine picture of a child made to look or act like an adult. How hard were these to find? How many were pictures of males? Females?

☑ The pro-incest view states incest is healthy and good. Such organizations believe children deserve the right to choose sexual partners and experiment. Discuss: When does experimentation or normal curiosity become abuse? Note: studies show that wide age differences, lack of mutuality, and use of force are some critical issues.

☑ Tell students to cut pictures from magazines that show males and females in sex-role stereotypic ways. Have them also cut out pictures that depict both sexes in non-traditional roles or making adult choices. Make contrasting bulletin board displays with words and images to depict this. How do students think stereotypic depictions can impact sexual abuse or sexual assault in society?

☑ Values Line — Compile a list of facts and misconceptions about child sexual abuse. Have one side of the room indicate "agree," the other side "disagree" and the middle "I don't know." Have students move to show their answers to your questions. You may want to try again after all your presentations to see if attitudes have changed and knowledge has been gained. This is especially useful around victim-blaming issues, what should happen to sex offenders, date-rape scenarios, drinking by the victim.

Blaming/Not Blaming the Victim

☑ Compare sexual assault of children or women with:

- getting a purse or wallet stolen;

- falling down a flight of stairs;

- a male being raped.

- Would people blame the victim more in one case than another? Are these fair comparisons?

☑ Have students write a letter to a person of their choosing as though they were victims of sexual abuse, disclosing, and requesting help.

☑ Have students answer their own or another's letter in a supportive/non-blaming manner. (A variation of this would be to write to Dear Abby, collect all problems in a box, and read them in class, providing answers as a group.)

☑ Students' debate panel — Choose three students to present an argument on an aspect of the problem and discuss. Two should have opposing views with one undecided. The following could be topics:

- The victim is never to blame.

- What should happen to offenders?

- Children are sexual beings and should be able to express that.

- Children often lie about sexual abuse and are not reliable witnesses.

- Religion can contribute to the occurrence and cover-up of incest.

☑ What about walking "sexy"? Remind the class that rape is an act of violence — not of sex. What kinds of internal attitudes, self-concepts, or messages do we communicate when we dress attractively or seductively? (Good feelings about ourselves, feelings of inadequacy, asking for attention, asking for affection, asking for affirmation, etc.) Are people who dress and walk seductively asking to be raped? (Be sure to point out that males as well as females dress and walk seductively.)

Community Resources

☑ Assign students to do research on local procedures when a child is a victim of incest or a victim of sexual assault by a stranger. What will likely happen, in what time frame, and what could be the outcome? Who is involved besides police, hospitals, and courts? Contrast and compare. Students working in committees could cover more ground, interview more authorities, etc.

☑ Invite a guest speaker from your local crisis hotline to explain services and handout crisis hotline cards for the students' further reference. Other speakers concerned with the problem of child sexual abuse may be medical professionals, welfare caseworkers, therapists, etc.

☑ Have students learn to write public service announcements, or do other community awareness activities in the school paper, radio, or TV station.

Role Plays*

Two prime components critical to successful sexual-abuse prevention are information and skills. Information may be transmitted in many ways, but skills are learned primarily through practice. The use of role plays and other theater techniques give adolescents a safe and effective opportunity to learn and exercise preventive skills.

A teacher or youth worker desiring to give adolescents this opportunity to improve prevention skills does not need to be skilled or experienced in acting or theater. Given a safe, open environment and enough information, most adolescents respond enthusiastically to a chance to pretend. The objective of this activity is not to coach the "actors" into polished performances, but simply to give them an opportunity to experiment and practice.

The following steps will help you encourage the participation of group members.

☑ Do not comment on an individual's performance as an actor. Evaluation should focus only upon their use of information and skills.

☑ A "creative" atmosphere needs to be established. A creative atmosphere is a balance between structure and freedom. Too much freedom leads to pandemonium. Too much structure stifles experimentation. Each leader will need to plan for and adjust to the needs of the specific group which she or he is leading. Some possibilities for encouraging structure and freedom are:

Structure

■ Recognition that personal safety is serious business.

■ A list of questions to be answered (perhaps on blackboard) and guidance from the leader when discussion strays from the questions.

■ Strict silence and attention from the audience when actors role play.

■ Desks clear of any unnecessary paper, pencils, or projects.

■ The room should be arranged so that everyone can see clearly, but there should be clear understanding when participants may move and when they must sit.

■ There can be a discussion about laughing or making fun of someone who is acting or answering questions. A leader should be sensitive to the difference between nervous or supporting kinds of laughter and laughter that hurts or stifles a participant.

---

*Developed by Don Yost and Carol Plummer, Bridgework Theater, Goshen, IN.

Freedom

- A leader's own attitude is usually the key to freeing up an atmosphere. A willingness to listen and give attention to every idea, no matter how silly it may sound at first is important. It says, "We are here to try things out, not to enforce or establish hard and fast rules."

- Trust is crucial to freedom and is a by-product of structure. Participants should trust that they will not be harassed or belittled for any reason, by classmates, but most importantly, by you, the leader.

- You will have some ideas of the right and wrong answers. Participants will need at some point to have firm ideas of safe and unsafe things to do in any given situation. However, labeling answers or actions in a play as "right" or "wrong" can inhibit a participant's willingness to venture guesses. A good technique for dealing with a "wrong" answer is to ask a question in return. For example:

Leader: *What should Brenda do when her date tries to touch her?*

Child: *Kick him in the _____.*

Leader: *Wait a minute. This is her date. She likes him but doesn't want to be sexual. What else could she say or do?*

- Give lots of positive reinforcement. Acting and answering can be frightening and participants may need lots of encouragement and reassurance that they are doing fine.

- Allow freedom to follow a line of questioning or discussion for which you may not be prepared, but which seems important to the participants.

- Answer and explain in a straightforward manner and to the best of your ability. If it is your opinion, let them know. If you don't know the answer, tell them that you will find out and be sure to report back.

☑ Role play is a specific technique, differing from theater in that the purpose has little to do with a performance or end product. Role play is valuable for the experience itself. People can experience emotions and situations unfamiliar to their own lives. Role play is not, however, improvisation, which at its extreme offers neither scripts, characters, nor settings. With role play, participants are usually assigned a character, history, and a setting. A participant in role play may also be given a script, or an outline of what to say. Many times creation of a dialogue is left up to the participants.

In the suggested role plays, participants are given a situation and a character. They are not given a script, but there are usually some suggestions of what to talk about and where the action should lead.

Role Play 1: "Developing Skills"

Goal: To develop skills in refusing sexual advances.

Procedure:

1. Ask the group to quickly identify some of the "come-on" lines used by people their own age. List both lines used by males and females. The group may tend to focus on lines used to suggest intercourse. See that they consider other sexual activity as well (kissing, close dancing, or petting).

2. Set up two chairs. Ask a male and a female to take a seat. Ask one of the two to pick out a couple of the lines the class has listed. The task of the second person is to refuse the suggested activity. The asker should continue to press the case making it as difficult as possible for the refuser to refuse. (No physical coercion.)

3. Ask the class to evaluate the attempts of the asker and of the refuser. What kinds of come-ons were hardest to refuse? ("Don't you love me?" "Don't you trust me?") What kinds of refusals worked best? (Assertive ones.)

4. Switch couples. The second couple should try different come-ons and assume different personalities.

5. (Optional) Assign or have the class assign roles which reflect an imbalance of power (see Role Play 5) such as a football star dating a wallflower or a 21-year-old dating a 16-year-old. How do different kinds of power make it harder or easier to refuse sexual advancement even though you are in a less powerful position? (Identifying or linking up with other sources of power . . . friends, parents, police, body rights, self-esteem, etc.)

6. Ask the class to list the reasons that people refuse sexual advances. List as many as possible. Are all of them fair or legitimate? Is there ever a time when one person has the right to go ahead and trick or force another person into sexual contact? What are some of the best or strongest reasons to refuse sexual advances? Why is it difficult to communicate these reasons to other people? (Afraid of hurting their feelings, afraid of looking stupid, frigid, or unloving. Confusion about exactly how much and what kinds of sexual contact we desire.)

7. Ask another student to play the asker. Ask several students to play the refuser . . . practicing and refining good ways to refuse. (See Step 5.)

Role Play 2: "Awareness"

Goal: To increase awareness of the different techniques used by sex offenders to force or trick the people they offend. To familiarize students with some of the dynamics of father-daughter incest.

Procedure:

1. Set up two chairs. Designate one as the father's chair. The second is the daughter's chair. The daughter is 14 to 16 years old.

2. Ask the class to assume that the father wants his daughter as a sexual partner. Depending on the comfort of the class with this issue, you may want to assign a less threatening kind of sexual activity that the father desires. For example, he wants her to leave the bathroom door open or wants her to model some revealing clothes for him but won't allow her to wear them outside of the house.

3. Ask two students to take the roles. Father should try to verbally coerce his daughter into the designated activity. The daughter should hesitate. The father will probably have difficulty finding lines. Sometimes it is best for a teacher to play these roles.

4. Suggest to the father that he bribe his daughter. Certain kinds of bribes may pop up easily. ("I'll let you stay out late." "I'll teach you or let you drive the car.") Suggest more subtle, more powerful kinds of bribes — affection, respect, tenderness. Discuss the victim's feelings.

5. Ask a second student to play a father who uses threats to get his way. Again, you may help to identify more subtle threats such as withholding affection, loss of affirmation, revealing secrets, or blackmail. Discuss the victim's feelings.

6. A third student can try a father who uses intimidation. Intimidation differs from threats in that the offender tries to emphasize a person's position of powerlessness (as a child, employee, small person, or a person without money). Discuss the victim's feelings.

7. Ask the class to identify aspects of a parent-child relationship that make it especially easy for a parent to force or trick a son or daughter into sexual activity. (Love, lust, obedience, extreme differences in power, or a desire to keep the family together and running smoothly.)

Note: In no way should this role play be "practicing" offender's techniques. The focus should be on the way these ploys make the victim feel and to build empathy from peers.

Role Play 3: "Support"

Goal: To identify and encourage attitudes and skills that will support people who have experienced sexual abuse.

Procedure:

1. Set up three chairs. In the middle chair, ask a student to play the part of a person who has been tricked or forced into sexual contact. If the person needs help, ask the class to quickly identify a few specifics of who, what, where, and when the abuse took place (or use a case study). This person should try to tell his or her friends about the incident.

2. In the other two chairs, ask one student to play the part of a friend who tries to be helpful and supportive. Ask the other student to play a friend who is not.

3. After the trio has spent a few minutes with the scene, ask the class to make suggestions to each friend. What are good ways to be of help? (Stay calm, serious, interested, believe it can happen, don't blame the victim, or encourage the victimized person to get help.) What are the most damaging things that the unsupportive friend can do? (Laugh, ridicule, disbelieve, embarrassment, gossip, condemn.)

4. If a female has played the part of the victimized person, try using a male. Ask the class to identify ways in which it is easier or more difficult to be both supportive or nonsupportive. Males may be especially vulnerable to accusations of homosexuality or being too weak to protect themselves. They may also feel greater pressure to accept any kind of sexual contact as "good." On the other hand, males are often more resistant to blaming themselves for what happened.

Role Play 4: "Reporting"

Goal: To develop skills and realistic expectations about reporting sexual abuse.

Procedure:

1. Ask a student to play a person who has been victimized. As in Role Play 3, the class may want to help decide a few of the specifics of the incident.

2. Ask four or five students to form a line at the front of the room. Ask the class to identify persons they might trust to help with a problem of sexual abuse (parents, counselor, friend, police, or teacher). Assign these roles to the students at the front of the class.

3. At this point, it might be helpful to ask the victim to leave the room. Instruct the people in the line that when the victim attempts to tell them of the abuse, all except the last one in line are to act in an unsupportive manner.

4. Ask the victim to attempt to tell the different people about his or her experience.

5. Yes, it's hard to tell but it's important to keep telling even if the person you tell isn't helpful or supportive.

Role Play 5: "Power in Relationships"

Goal: Increase awareness of how power functions in an abusive relationship.

Procedure:

1. Ask the class to list groups or kinds of people who are less powerful than they are. Accept all reasonable answers at first, but then push them to think about "local" examples — people with whom they have direct contact.

2. Make the same kind of list for persons who they feel are more powerful than they.

3. Make additions to these lists of persons more or less powerful than they but of the same general age. These additions will probably vary for each individual. Examples of more powerful people may be members of student council, football team, honor society or persons with powerful parents. Less powerful may include people with few friends, foster children, ugly people, those with low grades.

4. Choose an example from each column. Ask two students to play the people you have chosen. Ask one of the players (not necessarily the most powerful) to attempt to trick or force the other player into some kind of sexual contact using verbal coercion only. Allow only a minute or two.

5. Try several more combinations using different students playing varying roles. Discuss the power relationship of an offender's ability to trick or force and the victim's ability or range of choices in his or her attempt to prevent abuse.

6. Ask the class to list sources of power that have little or nothing to do with social position, background, physical size, or ability. (Self-esteem, self-confidence, humor, imagination, honesty, self-understanding, and especially previous education about and awareness of the dynamics of sexual abuse.)

7. Use two of the characters previously designated, but instruct the less powerful person to respond with these "internal" sources of power.

Role Play 6: "Prevention"

Goal: Increase awareness of options to prevent sexual abuse.

Procedure:

1. Set up two chairs. One chair will define the person who sits in it as the offender. The other chair will designate the victimized person. Ask two students to play the roles. Their task is to participate in a kind of "What if . . . ?" dialogue.

Example:

Offender: *What if I came up to you and whipped open my raincoat and I didn't have anything on underneath it?*

Victim: *Well, let's see. What if I turned around and ran in the opposite direction?*

Offender: *I might think you were afraid. What if I started running after you?*

Victim: *I'd really be scared then. What if I ran into the nearest house and locked the door?*

2. Keep in mind that the purpose of this dialogue is not to "win." The object is to explore realistic alternatives to possible situations. This likely prohibits the use of machine guns, helicopters, or Karate.

3. The rest of the class may act as referees by interrupting at points where it is felt that either victim or the offender is being unrealistic or at points where the victim is stuck and the referees have another option to offer. If the victim gets stuck, the class may also discuss the choice of options that lead to having no options left.

4. (Optional) Try different combinations of gender — two males, a female offender, two females. How does this change options? In case of same gender, it is important to point out that homosexuality is rarely the motivation of an offender. In most cases of same-sex offense, it is between an adult and a younger person. It is the youth of the victim that is important, not the gender.

5. Emphasize that "acting smart" or fast or tricky will not always prevent sexual abuse. This exercise is merely to expand options to help prevent assault. And if the person was too frightened to try all the options or prevention skills it still is not the fault of the victim.

Role Play 7: "Contrasting Behaviors"

Goal: To contrast assertive, aggressive, and passive responses to unwanted sexual advances on a date.

Procedure:

1. Ask for a male and a female volunteer for the role play.

2. Explain that the two chairs in which they're seated are the front seat of a car. The two have just seen a movie together. She wants to go straight home. He intends to go parking.

3. In the first role play, ask him to try to convince her to stay out with him a while longer. Have the female show a passive "no" response to his suggestion. (She might make excuses, lie, pretend, or manipulate, but won't just be firm and honest.)

4. Now have the two (or two other volunteer actors) model an aggressive interaction. The female may respond to the male's request by calling him names, insulting him, accusing him, or even pretending to hit him.

5. Finally, ask for an assertive response from the female to the same request. The message should be clear, direct, and firm. It should give consistent verbal and nonverbal messages, yet it need not be an attack.

Role Play 8: "Talking"

Goal: To practice talking to our "children" about prevention of child sexual abuse.

Procedure:

1. Select two volunteers for the role play. One will play the parent, one will play a second-grade child.

2. The second grader has come home from school with a story to tell the parent about the day's events. The teacher has told the class to come in from the playground because a "weird man" was seen nearby. The child is confused.

3. The parent decides to use this opportunity to tell the child not only about safety around strangers but about sexual abuse prevention even with non-strangers.

4. Take suggestions from the class if the "parent" gets stuck on what to say.

5. Role play using other students as parents depicting other situations to talk with children of varying ages.

Middle and High School Pre- and Post-Test

Date: _____

❑ Pre   ❑ Post

❑ Male   ❑ Female

Please complete this form to the best of your ability. Do not put your name on this. Although we want to know what you think, we do not need to know individual names, so you can be completely honest and we will keep everything confidential. Your answers will help us to make our program better for other teenagers. Thanks for your help. Remember to give only one answer for each question. If you decide not to participate in the evaluation, simply write "no" in each space reserved for an answer.

Please choose the one best answer for each question.

_____ 1. Sexual assault is:

     a. The same as rape.
     b. When you are touched sexually.
     c. Being forced or tricked into sexual contact.
     d. Getting beat up and raped at the same time.

_____ 2. Sexual assault happens because:

     a. One person wants to have power over another.
     b. One person wants sex and loses control.
     c. Some women lead men on by the way they dress and act.
     d. Victims become offenders who assault other people.

_____ 3. A victim is someone who gets hurt by a crime. Who are likely to be victims of sexual assault?

     a. Mostly boys and girls under the age of six.
     b. Mostly teenage females who dress seductively.
     c. Boys and girls of all ages.
     d. Mostly attractive children.

_____ 4. Who is to blame if someone sexually abuses a teenager?

     a. In cases where the adolescent leads on the adult, responsibility is shared.
     b. The abuser is always to blame.
     c. It is the abuser's fault unless the teen lets it happen repeatedly.
     d. If drugs or alcohol were used by the abuser, the substances probably made abuse happen.

_____ 5. What is one good rule that can help you to stay out of dangerous situations?

    a. Never go out after dark alone.
    b. Assert your boundaries.
    c. Avoid strangers.
    d. There is no way to stay out of dangerous situations.

_____ 6. Sexual assault (of youth aged 2-18) is usually committed by:

    a. Pedophiles, also known as "dirty old men."
    b. People the victim knows.
    c. People who are mentally insane.
    d. Alcoholics.

_____ 7. If a friend shared that she had been a victim of incest, what would be the best thing you could do?

    a. Tell a grownup right away.
    b. Discuss it with other friends to get more support and understanding for her.
    c. Encourage her to talk to a grownup and offer to go with her to tell them.
    d. Call the police so the offender can be arrested.

_____ 8. If you are ever sexually abused by an adult, the first person you tell:

    a. Will not believe you.
    b. Will be helpful.
    c. May not know how to help you.
    d. Will always make certain the abuse stops.

_____ 9. What should you do if you tell someone you had been sexually assaulted and they didn't believe you?

    a. Stay away from the person who assaulted you and it won't happen again.
    b. Try to convince the person because if they won't believe you probably no one else will.
    c. Try to forget it and get on with life.
    d. Tell someone else who can help you.

_____ 10. If someone attempts to sexually assault you, it would be your fault if you:

    a. Didn't trust your feelings and get out of a dangerous situation.
    b. Didn't assert your boundaries and tell them "no."
    c. Didn't attempt self-defense or at least scream for help.
    d. Sexual assault is never the fault of the victim.

11. If an adult touches you and you don't like it, you should:

   a. Tell him or her to stop it and never tell anyone about it.
   b. Not argue because he or she is an adult and knows best.
   c. Tell him or her you don't like it and tell another adult about it.
   d. Let him or her because he or she is bigger than you and could hurt you.

12. Someone who reports a sex offender:

   a. May have to go to jail.
   b. Needs support from family and friends.
   c. Usually will have his or her name printed in the paper.
   d. Usually has to go to a foster home, if under age 18.

13. In a high school with a minimum of 1,000 students how many probably have experienced some type of sexual abuse?

   a. One
   b. 100
   c. 40
   d. 20

14. To protect yourself from sexual assault:

   a. Learn self-defense.
   b. Trust your feelings in situations that don't "feel right."
   c. Try to never go out alone at night.
   d. Avoid contact with "questionable" people.

15. The best way to get over bad feelings after a sexual assault or harassment is to:

   a. Get some counseling from a trained person.
   b. Allow yourself to cry some, but forget it as soon as you can.
   c. Keep busy to block out the memory.
   d. Go back to all your old activities as though it never occurred.

Pre- and Post-Test Answer Key for Middle and High School Students

1. c   Not all sex is abuse nor is all abuse violent. Sexual assault usually involves at least verbal coercion or manipulation but need not include penetration. In fact, though the public sees penetration as more destructive, this is not the only important factor.

2. a   Sexual assault and harassment are issues of power and control. Sexual feelings do not make people's behaviors uncontrollable. Also, most victims *do not* grow up to be offenders, although many offenders were past victims.

3. c   It is a myth that good looking, seductively dressed teenagers attract abuse and are desirous of sexual experience. Offenders often use this excuse yet the average age of child victims is 8–11 years old. Boys and girls of all ages, shapes, and personalities are victimized.

4. b   While dressing seductively or being in certain places may not be wise, it does not justify sexual assault. And certainly no one should be blamed because they weren't clever enough to get away or if they were unsure how to get help once it started.

5. b   Children's bodies belong to them. There are limits and boundaries, even with relatives. Assertiveness skills are more realistic than avoidance or curtailed activity.

6. b   No more than 25 percent of offenders are strangers to their victims and there are no data saying most offenders are "dirty old men" or mentally disabled.

7. c   The offender may not go to jail and, often, if the victim is related, he or she may not make the report if jail is seen as the inevitable outcome. Do not take over, but *support* your friend in choosing to get help.

8. c   Children rarely lie about something as embarrassing and painful as sexual abuse. Exaggeration occur by saying it happens less or already ended when it may be frequent and regular occurrence. Though many adults may want to help, it is still sadly true that some are disbelieving and unhelpful.

9. d   Encourage youth to keep seeking help if they don't receive it at first and to get help to ensure their own as well as others' safety.

10. d   If fear or lack of knowledge keeps someone from using prevention skills, they should not blame themselves, but seek professional guidance and support.

11. c   It is usually best for the youth to both assert rights to his or her own body and tell another adult to make sure it stops.

12. b   Reporting is difficult when one is a victim and chooses to forget the bad experience.

13. b   Some studies even go further to say that up to 38 percent of all females are sexually abused before turning 18 years old, and approximately 15 percent of males are also victims.

14. b   Self-defense isn't for everyone and doesn't always work. In fact, it may bring added violence with certain offenders. Just restricting your activities or avoiding undesirables is also no sure-fire safeguard.

15. a   Most people need at least some crisis counseling after something as traumatic as sexual abuse. Forgetting is something most victims want to do but an unresolved problem could haunt them later in their relationships, sexual development, and self-concept.

Victims Panel Exercise

Note: This exercise may not be appropriate for immature middle-school students.

Goal: Increase peer support for victims. Increase understanding of sexual abuse dynamics. Increase understanding that victims are never to blame.

Procedure:

1. The four character descriptions at the end of this exercise are written in two paragraphs. The first is a superficial description of the character. The second is a more in-depth description of that character's reaction to an abusive situation.

2. Print each of the four descriptions on a separate sheet of paper. Be sure to change the names of the characters if they duplicate persons in the school or in your group. Ask for volunteers to serve as readers. Remember that some students may be or may have been victims themselves. You may want to assign the readings the day before the exercise so that readers have a chance to rehearse and become comfortable with the material.

3. The day of the exercise, ask all four readers to read their first paragraph to the class. Ask the class to discuss which of the four characters they think are most likely to be or to have been sexually abused. (This discussion may center on power and self-confidence.)

4. Ask each reader to read their second paragraph. After each reader has finished, ask the class for their comments. Were their guesses about the likelihood of abuse correct? How does knowing about the information contained in the second paragraph change their opinions about the character? What is the most helpful way to respond to each person? What actions would be especially hurtful?

5. There may be special questions about the fourth character. Did this person actually experience abuse? If so, whose fault was it? Again, ask the class to discuss harmful and helpful ways of responding.

Character Descriptions:

Sandy is a 15-year-old girl. She is a terror in school. She drinks, smokes, and chases boys. Sandy wears lots of make-up and ''sexy'' clothes. She has a bad reputation. She has no close friends. Even the people she hangs out with complain because she makes a lot of excuses to keep from becoming close friends. Sandy dates lots of boys, but never just one. She comes on to everybody — even teachers.

The reason behind all of this is that Sandy's father insists on having sexual contact with her. She is scared stiff that somebody will find out. The only affection she has ever received from a male was connected to sexual contact. Sandy feels she is tainted — that she is so dirty that no one would ever like her for anything but sex. The only way she knows of getting what she wants, including love and affirmation is through sex — because that's the way her father treats her.

Frances is 15. She is a straight-A student. She is a member of three different school clubs. Everyone thinks she will go on to get a scholarship to a big university. Hundreds of people voted for Frances as homecoming queen, but she really doesn't have any close friends. She has dated this one guy sort of off and on for a long time. She says she likes him because he doesn't ask too much — because he lets her be free.

The reason behind all of this is that Frances's father insists on having sexual contact with her. She is scared that someone will find out. She tries to do everything she can to hide, to pretend that nothing like this could ever happen to her. Frances is worried that the whole thing is her fault. Her dad says she is too pretty and that she tempts him too much. Frances feels like she has sinned. She tries hard to "make up" for it by doing everything right. At school she appears happy-go-lucky. At home she is depressed, angry, and confused. She is sure that no boy in his right mind would want to go out with her if he knew what was happening.

Jerry is 16. He plays defensive end on the football team. There are lots of girls who would like to go out with him, but he doesn't date much. Jerry feels left out. All the guys at school talk about everything they do with their girlfriends, but somehow, it never happened to Jerry. He feels like he missed the boat somewhere and that if he dates any girl for long, she will find out how ignorant he is and tell the whole world.

One day Jerry comes home from school to find that one of his mother's best friends is the only person home. The lady acts real strange. She tousles his hair and offers him a drink. When she hands him the glass, she rubs up against him. She talks a lot about how her husband can't please her. Jerry has the feeling that she is trying to get him to go to bed with her, but she makes him sick. He sure doesn't want to hurt her feelings or make her mad, because he knows she can tell his mother anything she wants to. Jerry's mother comes home before anything happens, but in the days that follow, he is really confused. He can't tell any of his friends because he thinks the guys would call him nuts for turning her down. He keeps thinking this is his one chance. He feels like a chicken and it starts to get depressing. He turns down some invitations to parties and can't concentrate on his homework. Jerry dreads the next time he has to face this woman alone.

Steve is 13. His dad is a policeman and loves football. Steve likes to draw. He draws things every chance he gets. Last year his dad made him go out for little league and he hated every minute of it. The first time he struck out, he couldn't help it, he cried.

Steve has an uncle who is single. This uncle has always taken Steve places. He is the only person Steve knows who will take him to the art museum. His uncle has always hugged and held him a lot. It's funny, because his dad never does. Steve's dad thinks hugging is "sissy" stuff. Steve's uncle has never done anything to make Steve feel hurt or sick inside or afraid, but one day Steve's dad gets really mad and calls him a "little homo." Steve starts thinking about himself and his uncle. He's afraid that maybe he is homosexual. Pretty soon Steve is afraid to talk with the guys at school or to take showers after gym class. Steve is really confused. He tries to find excuses for staying home from school. One day, he tries to run away.

Notes to Secondary Teachers

These are only a few topics to explore in relating the curriculum to your subject matter. The resources listed in Appendix J may also be helpful.

Family Life/Parenting Classes

1. The cycle of abuse from one generation to the next.

2. How and when to talk to your children about child sexual abuse.

3. Family dynamics in an incestuous family.

4. Helpful ways to respond if your child is molested.

5. How family systems therapy treats incestuous families.

6. Signs or indicators that your child or family may have a problem.

Social Studies/Sociology/Psychology

1. Types of offenders, their past, and their prognosis.

2. The history of child sexual abuse.

3. Society's contribution to the problem.

4. Victimology.

5. Future psychological or social problems resulting from being abused.

6. System Trauma (how social services can further hurt the victim).

7. Patriarchy and tolerance of child sexual abuse.

8. Contrast and compare rape and child sexual abuse.

9. In history, research famous leaders who were children of incest or who lived in adult incestuous relationships. How do you feel about this?

Health/Physical Education

1. Prevention as a safety issue.

2. Venereal disease contracted by child victims.

3. Sexual problems and confusion resulting from abuse.

4. Psychosomatic illness and other secondary health symptoms of abuse.

5. Reasons for higher rates of abuse of the physically or mentally handicapped.

Child Development

1. How abuse affects children differently based on age, length of abuse, relationship to offender.

2. Behavioral or physical signs of child sexual abuse.

3. The role of educators or parents in preventing abuse.

4. How does this relate to children's rights.

5. Why "special" children are more often abused — first born, twins, premature babies, disabled, exceptionally bright, etc.

6. Compare physical abuse, sexual abuse, and neglect.

English/Language Arts

1. Assign opinion papers, book reports, research papers, or oral reports on previously mentioned topics.

2. Bring up topics when reading *Oedipus Rex,* English Romantic authors, or other classics where incest or sexual abuse is mentioned.

Drama

1. Research could be done to write, individually or collectively, skits or a play about an aspect of child sexual abuse.

2. Encourage dramatic readings or role plays about this topic.

   Topics:

   - Characterizations of victims, offenders, or families.

   - Demonstrate how, to whom, and when to report abuse.

   - Ways to support a friend.

   - Educate the public about a problem with a skit.

3. Efforts could be made to combine the artistic medium with this or other topics of social concern such as spouse abuse, poverty, substance abuse, job problems, etc.

4. View and critique plays or videotapes, *Out of the Trap,* or other materials listed in Appendix J.

Case Studies

- **Ted,** 9 years old, lives with his father and two older brothers (15 and 17). His dad is always busy at work with lots of meetings afterwards. Ted freely runs the streets most of the late day and evening. He joins a little league team and becomes friends with his coach. His coach, Al, often takes Ted for a hamburger and a coke after practice and starts spending many free hours with him. Finally Al suggests to Ted, since they are such good friends, that they could get closer, and have a lot of fun as special friends. They could touch each other in intimate ways. Ted does not want to do this but feels trapped when Al threatens that he will tell his father that Ted has been stealing.

- **Tina** is 15 years old. Her father has been making sexual innuendos ever since her older sister ran away two years ago. He is now trying to force her into oral sex. He claims her mother won't believe her and they'll have to get a divorce if she tries to tell anyone. She feels scared, confused, and trapped. She loves her father, and doesn't want to hurt her mother or embarrass the family.

- **Scott,** 16, has problems at home. His parents are very strict and treat him like a child. He has no privacy. He has become good friends with Dave, an older man in his church. Scott spends more and more time at Dave's house. Dave lets Scott smoke and drink with him. (It's their secret.) Scott feels like an adult when he is with Dave. Dave has suggested that he and Scott become sexually involved. Scott thinks that people (parents) will wonder why they are not friends anymore if he refuses and stays away from Dave. And if he tells, they might think he is gay. Besides, they have their secrets as all good friends do.

- **Shari,** 9 years old, lives with her mother, father, and two brothers. Her mother has serious health problems and is often in the hospital. Dad has been sleeping with Shari for about a year since he doesn't want her in a room with her brothers. She often wakes up to find him touching her or masturbating in bed. He tells her there is nothing wrong with what they are doing since he is her father. He tells her, "How else will you learn about sexual things?"

- **Jerry** is on the starting five on the freshman basketball team. He looks older than his 14 years and is very proud of his muscles. One day the neighbor lady who is his mom's friend, asks Jerry to help her move in some furniture. Afterwards she comes on to him and invites him into her bedroom. He's confused and nervous and not sure what to do. His mom would never believe this. His buddies would think he was crazy for not messing around with her. But he's not into this kind of thing and it makes him feel upset.

- **Sue** is 12 years old. She is into drugs heavily and has problems at school. Her father had sexually molested her before her parents divorced. Her mother's live-in boyfriend raped Sue and is now up on charges. Sue realizes she relates only in sexual ways to men and wants to

145

change, but she just doesn't know how. She feels different from other girls her age. In fact, she feels "ruined."

■   **Jane** is 14 years old. She has run away from home to a big city. Now she is hungry and scared. She is taken in by a guy who feeds her and lets her sleep at his place. When she is on her feet again, she expresses a wish to go home. The guy refuses to let her go and says she owes him for the food and lodging. He forces her to prostitute herself for him. He hits her and sexually abuses her. She feels this is all her fault since she ran away from home in the first place.

Appendix A
Education for the Prevention
of Sexual Abuse Project

The concepts in this book were originally developed from the pioneering work done in the three years of this pilot project, called Education for the Prevention of Sexual Abuse (EPSA). This project was housed at Bridgework Theater in Goshen, Indiana.

History of this Child Sexual Abuse Prevention Project

The following phases are a summary of the program development:

1. Internal community awareness of the problem of child sexual abuse.

2. Research and identification of resources for preventive education.

3. Consultation and support from other prevention programs.

4. Purchase of services or products from other prevention programs.

5. Evaluation of our community's unique needs and options for a prevention program.

6. Creation and piloting of prevention program in our community.

7. Child sexual abuse prevention service is provided on a regular, ongoing basis in our community.*

In 1975 the local Women's Center began providing rape victims support. During 1977–78 the increased reporting of occurrences of child sexual abuse became a major community concern. In one week, four cases of child sexual abuse were reported to the local Youth Service Bureau, in this town with a population of only 43,000. In May 1978, the Youth Service Bureau invited persons to join an interagency task force to study the community situation and to recommend appropriate action. From this group's work and research, two local therapists were sent to Will County, Illinois, to receive incest treatment training. The Incest Treatment Program began at the Family Counseling Service in fall 1979.

The task force disbanded soon after the treatment program was in operation, but several members, concerned about prevention, created a new group, the Committee for the Prevention of Sexual Abuse (CPSA), including many of the original task force members. The new group, made up of representatives from counseling agencies, the police department, the rape crisis center,

---

*Phases adapted from a study by Illusion Theater.

youth-serving agencies, Child Protective Services, and school officials began meeting monthly beginning in March 1980.

Once focused on prevention, contact with Illusion Theater of Minneapolis (pioneers in the field of child sexual abuse prevention), became both natural and necessary for building our program. In the early fall of 1980, Cordelia Anderson from Illusion Theater presented a half-day conference sponsored by CPSA for community professionals and educators. In addition, the New Day Parent-Child Society, a local child abuse prevention agency, applied for a state grant for prevention of child sexual abuse. In the summer of 1980 that agency contracted with Bridgework Theater to write and produce *The Trial, the Mark, the Voice* as an educational theater piece geared to the general public.

By the time the National Center on Child Abuse and Neglect (NCCAN) put out requests for proposals for demonstrating approaches and effects of giving information to children about sexual abuse prevention, our community was ready to apply.

Education for the Prevention of Sexual Abuse (EPSA) was a program aimed at primary prevention of child sexual abuse, and accomplished through multiple activities operating simultaneously: heightening of general community awareness, promotion of professional and teacher training, development and testing of curriculum materials, play presentations to school-aged children, and parent education. The entire program relied upon an inter-agency advisory board/task force which met monthly to provide input and feedback to the EPSA project.

The design of the program was originally to provide impetus to Indiana communities, particularly the Elkhart County area, to begin and continue efforts to prevent child sexual abuse locally. After writing and testing curricula and plays with children and adults, these materials are now available for ongoing use in prevention. In the first three years, over 12,000 school-aged children participated in the project by either viewing a play and participating in a follow-up discussion, or through the use of the curriculum in their classroom.

Because of the importance of promoting public awareness of the problem, the EPSA project worked with the media in a variety of ways. Two plays were aired on local television stations and project staff participated frequently in radio and television programs on a statewide basis. Public support was also enhanced by over 50 newspaper articles explaining both the problem and our prevention program.

An impact study was conducted in conjunction with Graham McWhorter Research Associates to determine the responses of community leaders to our program. Eighty-two percent of the 60 respondents saw no negative effects from this prevention project. They indicated an ongoing need for this type of program to maintain awareness, help professionals, and help victims or potential victims. The most common suggestion for the project was to expand or extend the program (67 percent). Overwhelmingly, adults familiar with the prevention program were concerned that it should continue and spread to other communities as well.

Original EPSA Project Goals and Objectives

The EPSA goals and objectives are listed here to give you an idea of goals for prevention programs. They are not necessarily to be used as a blueprint, but to provide an example of what your community could try to accomplish. If you have adequate resources, you may choose a similar plan of action. Yet, even if you have far fewer resources, you may be able to pick and scale down some of these goals over a two-year period. There is no more important guidelines than to "begin where you are."

1. Expose at least 1,600 school-age children to information about sexual abuse in a comfortable manner and inform them on how to report and avoid such incidences.

2. Test and apply results towards improvement. Test methods of information delivery and apply results toward program improvement.

3. Train teachers of at least seven schools to be able to adequately detect and appropriately respond to and report instances of child sexual abuse.

4. Train volunteers and professionals statewide through the Indiana Chapter of the National Committee for the Prevention of Child Abuse in such form as seems most appropriate, including:

    ■ Five regional conferences

    ■ Produce a printed booklet of curriculum and inter-agency networking

    ■ Provide audio-visual aids — videotape and/or slide presentation

6. Integrate parts of our program into the public schools by making it a regular part of the ongoing curriculum.

7. Continue and further develop positive linkage between all agencies that come into contact with victims and/or offenders of child sexual abuse.

8. Educate the general community about the problem and need for positive prevention and treatment programs locally.

Appendix B
Sexual Abuse Fact Sheet

- Child sexual abuse is when someone is forced or tricked into sexual contact. This includes obscene phone calls, fondling, intercourse, anal or oral sex, prostitution, and pornography.

- Some experts estimate that five or six children in a typical classroom of 30 have been affected by sexual abuse, regardless of geographic area, race, or socioeconomic class.

- Ninety to 97 percent of abusers are men, at least in cases presently reported.

- Between 60 to 90 percent of victims of child sexual abuse are girls.

- Offenders are not usually strangers to children — 80 to 90 percent of offenders are known to children.

- The average length of an incestuous relationship is three years; it is rarely a one-time occurrence.

- The victim may cope in many ways: by being withdrawn, delinquent, or an over-achiever in school. Victims of sexual abuse are typically not as involved with their peers as other children.

- Emotional scars, not dealt with, may result in future problems with self-concept, and possibly violent or self-destructive tendencies.

- It is estimated that 28 million children will be sexually abused within the next decade.

- Studies indicate that between 12 and 38 percent of all women and 3 to 16 percent of all men experience some type of child sexual abuse.

- According to a 1984 study by Russell, only 5 percent of sexually abused girls ever report their abuse while a child.

- Living apart from biological parents increases the likelihood of sexual abuse for girls.

- Five studies document that a poor mother/daughter relationship increases the chance of a girl being sexually abused. Absence and mental illness may contribute.

- Up to 45 percent of incest offenders use force or the threat of force during an assault, although only 1 to 2 percent claim to be badly beaten or hit (Christiansen and Blake 1990).

- "Grooming" a child for sexual abuse is almost a universal phenomenon, where trust is first built up and then betrayed (Salter).

- Studies including over 5,000 offenders show there is no documentation of a "typical offender" nor is there a psychological test that reliably detects abusers (Myers 1989).

- More than half of 14-year-olds who have had sexual experience report being sexually abused (California Department of Health Services).

- More than three million cases of suspected abuse are reported every year in the U.S. Over 15 percent are for suspected sexual abuse.

- Between 44 and 70 percent of sexual abuse involves use of alcohol by the offender, victim, or both.

- Fifty percent of child victims are molested in their own homes or the home of the offender.

- One study found that in 70 percent of the cases where the women were battered, their children were being sexually abused.

- As many as 21 to 40 percent of sexual abuse victims may show no symptomology.

- Twenty-five percent of men in prison are there for criminal sexual offenses.

- Underreporting of abuse continues to be a problem.

Appendix C
Sexual Abuse Definitions

After discussing touch, remind children that some "bad" or "confusing" touch is a crime. At that time, some of these definitions may be helpful. Keep in mind that the facts are often less frightening to the children than the fantasy or fears of what terms might mean.

Crime: Something that is against the law. More advanced: We as people in this society have decided it's not beneficial to either individuals or our population as a whole.

Victim: The person who gets hurt by a crime. This could be by losing property or getting physically or emotionally hurt.

Offender: The person who hurts someone else. The person who does the crime.

Sexual Assault: When you are forced, tricked, or confused into touching parts of another person or letting them touch you when you don't want to. (We sometimes demonstrate by saying "No one has the right to touch you here, here, or here," while covering with our hands our chest, pubic area, and buttocks.) For more advanced: Sexual assault is when someone is forced or tricked into sexual contact. It includes rape, incest, fondling, obscene phone calls, pornographic pictures of children, child prostitution, etc.

Obscene Phone Call: A call made to scare or upset the person who answers. Sometimes the person will breathe loud, talk dirty, or suggest sexual contact.

Exposer: Usually a male who wants to scare or shock people by showing them his penis (or between his legs, or "private parts").

Rape: When one person forces or tricks another in sexual intercourse. For less advanced students, the definition of sexual assault may be adequate. They usually have heard of rape but may think it is nudity, kidnapping, stealing, murder, or a bizarre combination of these. For more advanced students, you may state it could be vaginally, orally, or anally.

Acquaintance Rape: The act of rape when the offender is known to the victim and perhaps even a friend or a date.

Incest: Sexual contact between family members. Both victims and offenders can be either male or female. Most known incest is between adult males and female children or sibling. For less advanced: The person who sexually abuses could be someone you know, even someone you live with and love. We have found that children who are victims know exactly what is meant by this and those who are not will not be frightened into thinking all fathers or grandfathers are abusive.

Privacy: The right to be alone or to have things that we don't share with others. For example, we don't need to let others read our diary or watch us when we are undressed.

Sexual Harassment: When one person makes sexual comments or touches, knowing the other does not want such attention. Often it is persistent and may be upsetting enough to disturb one's performance at work or school. Most jobs and schools now have policies prohibiting sexual harassment and telling one how to make complaints.

Appendix D
The Touch Continuum*

No Touch	Good Touches	Confusing Touches	Bad Touches	No Touch
	examples:	examples:	examples:	
	kiss	unexpected hug	hit	
	hug	tickling	slap	
	handshake	pat on rum	kick	
	pat on back	wrestling	being trapped	
	back rub	kiss	bite	

This continuum can be written on the board and discussed at various levels of sophistication, depending on the age of the students. Options include:

More Advanced

1. List their examples of touch and discuss.
2. Bad touch is better than touch deprivation.
3. Kisses, back rubs, and certain other touches can be bad or confusing.
4. Many confusing touches make us feel guilty because of distrust of our responses.
5. Confusing touch is often sexual in nature.
6. All types of touch could be role played.
7. Different cultures or individuals interpret touch differently.

Less Advanced

1. We all want and need touch
2. List their examples of types of touch.
3. Help each make own touch line to take home and stress individual differences.
4. Talk about being tricked and trapped as confusing.
5. Stress that they discuss with a trusted adult whenever they feel confused about touch.
6. No one has a right to touch you if you don't want to be touched.

*Used by permission of Illusion Theater, Inc., Minneapolis, Minn. The Touch Continuum: Originally developed by Cordelia Anderson in Minnesota, the concept of the "touch continuum" has been a staple of sexual abuse prevention programs since the late 1970s. While it has sometimes been oversimplified in listing what are "good" touches versus "bad" touches, the touch continuum is a valuable tool in helping people talk about the range of touches, including touch deprivation and painful or positive touches. It helps people to individualize the subjective experience of touch, recognizing the crucial variables of timing, context, relationship to the toucher, and emotional response. It validates that cultural and societal and family mores also influence our reaction to touch.

Appendix E
Options Chart*

Possible Examples:	What I'd Do	What's the Worst that Can Happen	What's the Best that Can Happen	What's Most Likely to Happen
In case of abuse	Hit	Get beat up or killed	He could be surprised and leave	Get hit back
	Run	Followed and caught	Get away	If someone's close, run to them
	Agree for now, tell later	Be abused, physically and sexually	Offender wouldn't do anything much	Offender will do more than child feels good about
After abuse	Tell	Not be believed	Get support	Keep telling until someone believes
	Not tell	Abuse gets worse	Abuse will disappear	Abuse will continue
	Try to forget	Sibling gets abused next	Never think of it again	Nightmares — fears of recurrence

Situations:

1. Joe is eight years old. He notices someone following him home from school. The man is a stranger, but clean and well-dressed.

2. Nancy's stepfather is always telling her how pretty she is and telling her dirty jokes. She is 13. Lately he tries to kiss her on the lips and she feels uncomfortable.

3. The man at the ice cream shop has made friends with 11-year-old Doris. He picks her up after school sometimes and says they're good enough friends to have some "special secrets," which even her parents can't know.

4. Dave's pastor supervises the youth group. Dave once stole money and the pastor promised not to tell his parents if he'd only touch him "down there." Dave didn't want to, but was scared, so did it. Now Dave feels like he can't tell or his parents would punish him for stealing.

---

*This can be used by making a chart or overhead with the category heads filled in. Students can give their own options in whatever situation is read. You may use their examples or ones you create, whatever is more appropriate for the group.

Appendix F
Prevention Skills

A. **Trust Your Feelings** — Many children are overly trusting of adults and obey even if something doesn't feel right to them. Or they don't leave a situation when they're nervous or afraid because it may just be "my imagination" or paranoia. Or they may have delusions that nothing could happen to them or that they could just beat up the person or outwit them.

B. **Be Aware of Your Environment** — Not being alert or being self-absorbed may actually attract an offender. Note if people are around, if someone is following you, etc. Make wise decisions so as not to further endanger yourself. Try not to hitchhike, for example, or be alone in a strange place at night.

C. **Assert Your Boundaries** — Define your boundaries. Stress that youth both have a right and a responsibility to know when, how, and by whom they will be touched. Each of us needs our own space, our own privacy. Usually others want to know our limits so that they can respect them.

Know the difference between assertive, aggressive, and passive behaviors and how behavior affects others.

- Passive — These people don't know or at least don't state clearly what they want. They beat around the bush or give hints.

- Aggressive — These people push their needs to the degree that they may hurt other people, physically or emotionally. By considering only their own needs they may often get hurt physically or emotionally by others in response.

- Assertive — These people respect their own rights as well as the rights of others. They are tactful but very direct about their needs.

- For very young children, emphasize communication. If they feel confused, that is enough reason to tell a trusted adult what has happened.

- Never is a child or youth to blame for abuse even if they don't know about or use prevention skills, or if the skills don't work.

D. **Additional Safety Tips**

- Have a heightened general self-awareness. This can show in how you walk, if you seem to have a sense of purpose, if you are spaced out, if you don't seem to know the area, or if you don't seem aware of your surroundings.

- Keep a distance from people that you feel most uncomfortable with. Step back, be assertive, tell the person to leave, establish firmness with eye contact.

- Don't be embarrassed to follow your own best instincts. If the person following you makes you uncomfortable, cross the street or go into a store. Better silly (and safe) than sorry.

- Walk in the middle of the sidewalk. It's safer because you are less easily pulled into cars or alleys.

- Always lock your cars and house when you leave. We all should know this rule by now.

- Stay around other people, in public places, especially if you are feeling afraid or uneasy. Take a "buddy" when you go places because sometimes there really is safety in numbers.

- Stay as calm as you can if you are attacked so you can use your brain. The assailant is afraid, too, and may overreact to your responses.

- Scream and make a scene if you are near any houses, buildings, or in a public area. It can be very effective.

Resources

Personal — Have students list, perhaps on the back of their crisis hotline cards, the names of specific people they could talk to about any type of problem. Stress that it may be persons they like, trust, who will believe them, and are old enough to be able to help them solve the problem. Suggest also persons such as teacher, clergy, school counselor, scout leader, or doctor. In certain situations children feel they cannot tell family members, so lists should include at least one non-family person.

Community — Community resources vary from place to place, but there will be something available to you.

List your local resources: Crisis Hotline _____

Rape Support Center _____

Child Protective Services _____

Mental Health Center _____

Other Counseling _____

Police Department _____

Appendix G
Incest Indicators

While no set of facts will be totally definitive or apply completely to any one incestuous family, there are some similar dynamics in many cases. Most of the indicators listed below apply to father/daughter (including father/stepdaughter) incest which is the type reported most often.

Confusion of Boundaries

- Sometimes mothers and daughters operate on a peer level or even in role reversal. Daughter may take care of mother, care for other children, shop, clean, and even cook, in a primary way.

- Attitudes on nudity and sexual matters may either be repressed or overly expressed. For example, highly religious families that never discuss sex or allow any nudity may be abusive. Overly open persons who may regularly appear nude with children, have intercourse in front of them, sleep in a "family bed," etc., also may be abusive.

- Both parents and children may have difficulty in determining where they end and the other person begins. Both may think that the child's body is property of the parent.

Crisis Period

- Marriage problems where communication is not optimal, mother may be pregnant, sick, or work another shift, increase the likelihood for abuse. There may be spouse abuse as well. Or there may be no mother in the family at all due to death or divorce.

- Financial problems and unemployment, with the resulting low self-concept and identity problems can increase stress, and increase the likelihood of abuse.

- Substance abuse problems — 44 percent of the offenses of child sexual abuse occur while the offender is under the influence of alcohol or drugs which break down natural restraint. Other social relationships in the community tend to be poor as well.

High-Risk Groups

- Extreme isolation plays a factor. Girls from isolated rural homes are two and one-half times more likely to be victims than girls living in urban areas. Such families are often extremely ingrown and relate to few outside their family circle.

- Special children such as first born, premature babies, and the especially bright are all high risk. Disabled children, both physically or mentally, are at least twice as likely as others to be victims of sexual abuse.

- Family history of offenders usually includes either the observation or experience of some sexual abuse in their family of origin.

Fears of Disclosure

- Fear of family break-up through divorce or by the victim being placed in a foster home or institution is an important deterrent to disclosure.

- Fear of prison for the offender. Even the victim often does not want this outcome. Loss of income can be a real family consideration if the offender is the bread winner.

- Fear of being disowned by the family deters disclosure. Everyone feels guilty about not stopping the abuse — the victim, parents, and siblings. The victim and the offender both intensely fear family rejection.

- Fear of further abuse deters disclosure. All members of the family fear this even if they seek help. But if the problem is denied and no help is found, the abuse will probably continue and perhaps even become abusive in other harmful ways to the victim. Or, if he or she leaves the situation, chances are good that another child (or many children) may be sexually abused.

- Fear of harm to self or loved ones due to threats or implied threats is all too common. Frequently children have believed that they, a pet, or a parent will be injured or even killed by the offender if they tell about the abuse.

Appendix H
Reporting Child Sexual Abuse

Teachers often feel confused about under what circumstances and with what procedures sexual abuse should be reported. Although we feel confused, the question should not be if we should report (legally and morally we are required to), but rather how to report. Find out about your school policy which often has standard guidelines as to who and how the formal report should be made.

When to Report

In all states, teachers, parents, administrators, nurses, social workers, and concerned citizens must legally report any suspicion of child sexual abuse. Fortunately, we do not need to investigate the reality of that suspicion. Protective Services of the Department of Social Services or Family Independence Agency is legally mandated to do such an investigation. We should also keep in mind that according to federal legislation (Public Act 93-247, January 31, 1974), each state must "have in effect a state child abuse and neglect law which includes provision for immunity for persons reporting . . . from prosecution . . ." and that the report will be kept confidential.

Guidelines for reporting:

1. Whenever children tell you that they have had sexual contact with an adult (person over 18 years old), including:

    ■ Intercourse

    ■ Fondling or touching

    ■ Anal or oral sex

    ■ Used sexually in photographs, films or video

2. Whenever children tell you they have been forced or tricked into sexual contact with another child (particularly a child four or more years older, or a child 16-18 years old).

3. Whenever friends or acquaintances of a suspected victim report to you that the child has reported such abuse to them.

4. When physical evidence of sexual abuse is discovered (physical harm or irritation in genital areas or VD). It is crucial to understand that the majority of sexual abuse cases, especially where no insertion occurs, will have no medical evidence.

5. When a cluster of behaviors that could be indicative of abuse are observed, even without a direct statement about abuse, you may report suspicions to CPS (and they may or may not investigate depending on their evaluation of the likelihood of abuse).

Be aware of the following indications that sexual abuse may have been or may be going on.

1. Sudden change in mood or personality.

2. Sudden change in school performance.

3. Extreme withdrawal from social contacts with peers.

4. Acting out behaviors — fighting, exhibitionism, drug usage, runaways.

5. Seductive behaviors — learned from being used sexually.

6. Aversion to touch or closeness. Listlessness.

7. Psychosomatic illnesses.

8. Unusually fearful and distrustful of adults.

9. Overly compliant in attempts to please adults.

10. Lying or stealing.

11. Sexual preoccupation including sexual experimentation with other children, excessive masturbation, overly sexualized language themes, knowledge of sex beyond age expectations.

None of these behaviors alone are indicators of sexual abuse and, indeed, can be symptoms of other problems. However, concerns about a number of these may warrant more concerns and a potential referral.

How to Report

If you have questions about reporting or need additional information, contact your child protective services unit, department of social services. Please report situations as soon as possible to facilitate services to children and families. Report even if the child states the abuse has ended or that they have already told someone about it. Protective services' trained staff will do the investigation.

Your local child protective service number is _____

Appendix I
What Happens When a Report Is Made?

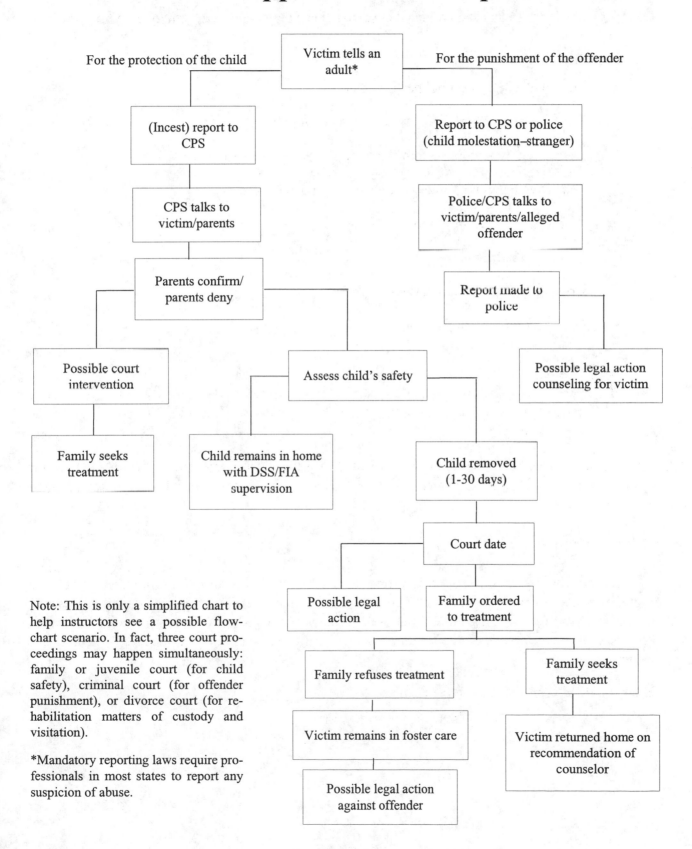

Victim tells an adult*

For the protection of the child

For the punishment of the offender

(Incest) report to CPS

Report to CPS or police (child molestation–stranger)

CPS talks to victim/parents

Police/CPS talks to victim/parents/alleged offender

Parents confirm/ parents deny

Report made to police

Possible court intervention

Assess child's safety

Possible legal action counseling for victim

Family seeks treatment

Child remains in home with DSS/FIA supervision

Child removed (1-30 days)

Court date

Possible legal action

Family ordered to treatment

Family refuses treatment

Family seeks treatment

Victim remains in foster care

Victim returned home on recommendation of counselor

Possible legal action against offender

Note: This is only a simplified chart to help instructors see a possible flow-chart scenario. In fact, three court proceedings may happen simultaneously: family or juvenile court (for child safety), criminal court (for offender punishment), or divorce court (for rehabilitation matters of custody and visitation).

*Mandatory reporting laws require professionals in most states to report any suspicion of abuse.

Appendix J
Child Sexual Abuse Books, Videotapes and Films, Plays, Cooperative Games, and Miscellaneous Materials

Books

For Teachers, Parents, and Concerned Adults of Sexually Abused Youth

Adams, Caren, and Jennifer Fay. *Nobody Told Me it Was Rape*. Santa Cruz, CA: Network Publications, 1984.

————. *No More Secrets: Protecting Your Child From Sexual Abuse*. San Luis Obispo: Impact Publishers, 1981.

Adams, Caren, Jennifer Fay, and Jan Loreen-Martin. *No Is Not Enough: Helping Teenagers Avoid Sexual Assault*. San Luis Obispo: Impact Publishers, 1984.

Armstrong, Louise. *Kiss Daddy Goodnight: A Speakout on Incest*. New York: Hawthorne Books, 1978; Pocket Books, 1979.

Bass, Ellen, and Laura Davis. *The Courage to Heal: A Guide for Women Survivors of Child Sexual Abuse*. New York: Harper Row Publishers, 1988.

Bass, Ellen, and Louise Thorton, eds. *I Never Told Anyone: Writings by Women Survivors of Child Sexual Abuse*. New York: Harper Row Publishers, 1983.

Bateman, Py, and Gayle Stringer. *Where Do I Start? A Parent's Guide for Talking to Teens About Acquaintance Rape*. Seattle: Alternatives to Fear, 1984.

Briere, John, Berliner, Lucy, Buckley, Josephine, Jenny, Carole, and Theresa Reid, eds. *The APSAC Handbook on Child Maltreatment*. Thousands Oaks, CA: Sage Publications, 1996.

Bulkley, Josephine, Jo Ensminger, Vincent J. Fontana, and Roland Summitt. *Dealing with Sexual Child Abuse*. Chicago: National Committee for Prevention of Child Abuse, 1983.

Burgess, Ann Wolbert, A. Nicholas Groth, Lynda Holstrom, and Suzanne M. Sgroi. *Sexual Assault of Children and Adolescents*. Lexington: Lexington Books, 1978.

Butler, Sandra. *Conspiracy of Silence: The Trauma of Incest*. San Francisco: New Glide Publications, 1978; New York: Bantam Books, 1979.

Byerly, Carolyn M. *The Mother's Book: How to Survive the Incest of Your Child*. Dubuque, IA: Kendall/Hunt Publishing Co., 1985.

Colao, Flora, and Tamar Hosansky. *Your Children Should Know*. New York: Bobbs-Merrill Company, 1983.

Crewdson, John. *By Silence Betrayed: Sexual Abuse of Children in America*. Boston: Little, Brown, and Company, 1988.

Daugherty, Lynn. *Why Me? Help for Victims of Child Sexual Abuse (Even if They are Adults Now)*. Racine, WI: Mother Courage Press, 1984.

Finkelhor, David. *Child Sexual Abuse*. New York: The Free Press, 1984.

———. *Sexually Victimized Children*. New York: The Free Press, 1979.

Gil, Eliana. *Outgrowing the Pain: A Book for and about Adults Abused as Children*. Rockville, MD: Launch Press, 1983.

Hagans, Kathryn B., and Joyce Case. *When Your Child Has Been Molested: A Parent's Guide to Healing and Recovery*. Lexington, MA: Lexington Books, 1988.

Hechinger, Grace. *How to Raise a Street Smart Child*. New York: Hechinger, 1984.

Hillman, Donald, and Janice Solek-Tefft. *Spiders and Flies: Help for Parents and Teachers of Sexually Abused Children*. Lexington, MA: Lexington Books, 1988.

Horowitz, Robert M. *The Legal Rights of Children*. Monterey: Shepard's McGraw-Hill 1984.

Hyde, Margaret O. *Sexual Abuse: Let's Talk About It*. Philadelphia: Westminster Press, 1984.

Kent, Jack. *There's No Such Thing as a Dragon*. New York: Western Publishing Co., 1975.

King County Rape Relief. *He Told Me Not to Tell*. Renton, WA: King County Rape Relief, 1979. Distributed by Network Publications, Santa Cruz, CA.

Kraiser, Sherryl L. *The Safe Child Book*. New York: Dell Publishing Co., 1985.

Lerner, Harriet Goldhor. *The Dance of Anger*. New York: Harper and Row Publishers, 1985.

Mendel, Matthew Parynik. *The Male Survivor: The Impact of Sexual Abuse*. Thousand Oaks, CA: Sage Publications, 1995.

Myers, John E. B. *The Backlash: Child Protection Under Fire*. Thousand Oaks, CA: Sage Publications, 1994.

Rush, Florence. *The Best-Kept Secret*. Englewood Cliffs: Prentice-Hall, 1980.

168

Russell, Diana E. H. *The Secret Trauma: Incest in the Lives of Girls and Women.* New York: Basic Books, 1986.

———. *Sexual Exploitation: Rape, Child Sexual Abuse and Workplace Harassment.* Los Angeles: Sage Publications, 1984.

Sanford, Linda. *Come Tell Me Right Away.* Fayetteville, New York: Ed-U Press, 1982.

———. *The Silent Children: A Parent's Guide to the Prevention of Child Sexual Abuse.* New York: McGraw-Hill, 1980.

Seattle Rape Relief. *Choices: Sexual Assault Prevention for Persons with Disabilities.* Seattle, 1985.

Tobin, Pnina, and Susan Levinson Farley. *Keeping Kids Safe: A Child Sexual Abuse Prevention Manual.* Holmes Beach, FL: Learning Publications, 1990.

For Adolescents

Fink, Marjorie. *Adolescent Sexual Assault and Harassment Prevention Curriculum.* Holmes Beach, FL: Learning Publications, 1995.

Lee, Sharice. *The Survivor's Guide: For Teenage Girls Surviving Sexual Abuse.* Safe Publications, 1995.

Scott, Sharon. *How to Say No and Keep Your Friends — Peer Pressure Reversal for Teens and Preteens.* Amherst, MA: Human Resource Development Press, 1986.

Simon, Toby, and Bethany Golden. *Dating: Peer Education for Reducing Sexual Harassment and Violence Among Secondary Students.* Holmes Beach, FL: Learning Publications, 1996.

Simon, Toby, and Cathy Harris. *Sex Without Consent: A Peer Education Training Manual for Secondary Schools.* Holmes Beach, FL: Learning Publications, 1993.

For Children

Amerson, Ruth. *Hi! My Name is Sissy.* Sanford, NC: Department of Social Services, 1984.

Bass, Ellen. "I Like You to Make Jokes with Me, But I Don't Want You to Touch Me." In *Stories for Free Children.* Letty Cottin Pogrebin, ed. New York: McGraw-Hill, 1982.

Bassett, Kerry. *My Very Own Special Body Book.* Redding, CA: Hawthorne Press, 1980.

Bateman, Py. *Acquaintance Rape: Awareness and Prevention for Teenagers.* Seattle: Alternatives to Fear, 1982.

Berg, Eric. *Stop It!* Santa Cruz, CA: Network Publications, 1985.

———. *Tell Someone!* Santa Cruz, CA: Network Publications, 1985.

———. *Touch Talk!* Santa Cruz, CA: Network Publications, 1985.

Berry, Joy. *Alerting Kids to the Dangers of Sexual Abuse.* Waco, TX: Word, 1984.

C.A.R.E. *Trust Your Feelings.* Surrey, BC: C.A.R.E. Productions, 1984.

Coalition for Child Advocacy. *Touching.* Bellingham, WA: Whatcom County Opportunity Council, 1985.

Dayee, Frances. *Private Zone.* Washington: The Charles Franklin Press, 1982.

Ezsrine, Linda. *Anna's Secret.* Baltimore: Harvey S. Spector Publishing Co., 1985.

Freeman, Lory. *It's My Body.* Seattle: Parenting Press, 1982.

Gordon, Sol, and Judith Gordon. *A Better Safe Than Sorry Book.* Fayetteville, NY: Ed-U Press, 1984.

Hindman, Jan. *A Very Touching Book.* Durkee, OR: McClure-Hindman, 1983.

Kaufman, Gerhen and Lev Raphael. *Stick Up for Yourself!* Minneapolis: Free Spirit Publishing, 1990.

King County Rape Relief. *Top Secret.* Renton, WA: King County Rape Relief, 1982.

Mackey, Gene, and Helen Swan. *The Wonder What Owl.* Leawood, KS: Children's Institute of Kansas City, 1984.

Marvel Comics and National Committee for Prevention of Child Abuse. *Spider Man and Power Pack.* New York: Marvel Comics Group, 1984.

McGovern, Kevin B. *Alice Doesn't Babysit Anymore.* Portland: McGovern & Mulbacker Books, 1985.

Montgomery, Becky, Carol Grimm, and Peg Schwandt. *Once I Was a Little Bit Frightened.* Fargo, ND: Rape and Abuse Crisis Center, 1983.

Morgan, Marcia K. *My Feelings.* Eugene, OR: Equal Justice, 1984. Distributed by Network Publications, Santa Cruz, CA.

Morrison, Kenneth and Marcia Thompson. *Feeling Good About Me.* Minneapolis: Educational Media Corporation, 1985.

Neiburg, Terkel, Susan and Janice E. Rench. *Feeling Safe Feeling Strong: How to Avoid Sexual Abuse and What to Do It It Happens to You.* Minneapolis: Lerner Publications Company, 1984.

Palmer, Pat. *Liking Myself.* San Luis Obispo: Impact Publishers, 1982.

——. *The Mouse, the Monster and Me.* San Luis Obispo: Impact Publishers, 1977.

Renard, Sue and Kay Sockol. *The Collaborative Process: Enhancing Self-Concepts through K-6 Group Activities.* Minneapolis: Educational Media Corporation, 1993.

Stowell, Jo, and Mary Dietzel. *My Very Own Book About Me.* Spokane: Lutheran Social Services, 1982.

Sweet, Phyllis E. *Something Happened to Me.* Racine, WI: Mother Courage Press, 1981.

Terkel, Susan Neiburg, and Janice E. Rench. *Feeling Safe Feeling Strong.* Minneapolis: Lerner Publications Company, 1984. Distributed by Network Publications, Santa Cruz, CA.

Wachter, Oralee. *No More Secrets for Me.* Boston and Toronto: Little, Brown, and Company, 1982.

Wheat, Patty. *The Standoffs.* Torrence, CA: Parents Anonymous, 1980.

White, Laurie A., and Steven L. Spencer. *Take Care with Yourself.* Michigan: DayStar Press, 1983.

Williams, Joy. *Red Flag, Green Flag People.* Fargo, ND: Rape and Abuse Crisis Center, 1980.

YWCA. *You Belong to You: A Coloring Book.* Flint, MI: YWCA Sexual Assault Crisis Center, 1980. (Available in Spanish.)

Videotapes and Films

For Adults or Adolescents

Acquaintance Rape Prevention Series. MTI Teleprograms (multi-media package).

Aware and Not Afraid. Distributed by Migima Designs (video, 20 minutes, color).

Better Safe than Sorry I. Filmfair Communications (16mm and videocassette, 14 minutes).

Better Safe than Sorry III. Filmfair Communications (16mm and videocassette, 19 minutes, color).

Best Kept Secret. Motorola Teleprograms (16mm and videocassette, 15 minutes).

Boys Beware. AIMS Media (16mm and videocassette, 14 minutes).

Broken Dreams: The Secret of Dating Violence. Duluth Women's Coalition (70-slide presentation with sound track and discussion booklet).

Breaking Silence. Future Educational Films (color, 16mm and videocassette, 58 minutes).

Child Abuse. AIMS Media (color, 16mm and videocassette, 29 minutes).

Child Abuse. Society for Visual Education (color filmstrips, 12 minutes).

Child Abuse: Don't Hide the Hurt. AIMS Media (color, 16mm and videocassette, 12 minutes).

Child Molestation: A Crime Against Children. AIMS Media (16mm and videocassette, 11 minutes, color).

Child Molestation: When to Say No. AIMS Media (16mm, 13 minutes, color).

Child Sexual Abuse: What Your Children Should Know. Indiana University Audio-Visual Center (videocassette and 16mm).

Don't Get Stuck There. Boy's Town Center (15 minutes, color).

Double Jeopardy. MTI Teleprograms (16mm film, 40 minutes, color).

Girls Beware. AIMS Media (16mm and videocassette, 12 minutes).

Incest: The Victim Nobody Believes. Motorola Teleprograms (color, 16mm and videocassette, 23 minutes).

Investigation of Rape. Motorola Teleprograms (color, 20 minutes).

It's OK to Say No! Migima Designs (videocassette, color).

Killing Us Softly. Cambridge Documentary Films (16mm, color, 28 minutes).

Little Bear. The Bridgework Theater (videotape).

More than Friends. ODN Productions (videocassette in sign language, 21 minutes).

A Night Out. ODN Productions (videocassette in sign language, 10 minutes).

No Easy Answers. Indiana University Audio-Visual Center (3/4" videocassette, 50 minutes).

No More Secrets. ODN Productions (16mm, color, 13 minutes).

Not Only Strangers. Coronet Films and Video (16mm and video, 23 minutes, color).

Out of the Trap. Available from Bridgework Theater (video, 40 minutes, color).

Rape: A New Perspective. Motorola Teleprograms (color, 7 minutes).

Shatter the Silence. Phoenix Films (color, 16mm, videocassette, 29 minutes).

This Film is About Rape. Motorola Teleprograms (16mm, color, 30 minutes).

Touch. Motorola Teleprograms (16mm and videocassette, color, 32 minutes).

Twice a Victim. Kidsrights Catalog (video, 23 minutes).

For Children

Bellybuttons are Navels. Multi-Focus (16mm, 12 minutes, color

Better Safe than Sorry II. Filmfair Communications (16mm and video-cassette, 14 minutes).

Little Bear Teacher/Leader Training, Bridgework Theater (video, 30 minutes).

Scared Silent. Hosted by Oprah Winfrey, Kidsrights Catalog.

Some Secrets Should be Told. Motorola Teleprograms (16mm and video, 12 minutes).

Sometimes I Need to Say No. Rape Crisis Center of Syracuse (16mm, 35 minutes).

Strong Kids, Safe Kids. Paramount Studios (videocassette, color).

What is Sexual Harassment? Kidsrights Catalog (video, 23 minutes)

What Tadoo. Motorola Teleprograms (16mm and videocassette, color, 18 minutes).

Who Do You Tell? Motorola Teleprograms (16mm and 3/4" videocassette, color, 11 minutes).

Plays

Everybody's Business. Illusion Theater Peer Education Program (grades 7–12 performance level, 60 minutes).

Little Bear Program, Bridgework Theater (grades K-4).

No Easy Answers. Illusion Theater Peer Education Program (grades 7–12 performance level).

Peace Up! Illusion Theater Peer Education Program (grades 3–6 performance level).

Talk It Out. Illusion Theater Peer Education Program (grades 7–12 performance level).

Touch. Illusion Theater Peer Education Program (grades 3–6 performance level).

Cooperative Games

Butler, Susan. *Non-Competitive Games for People of All Ages.* Minneapolis: Bethany House Publishers, 1986.

Peyser Hazouri, Sandra and Miriam McLaughlin. *Warm Ups and Wind Downs: 101 Activities for Moving and Motivating Groups.* Minneapolis: Educational Media Corporation, 1993.

Miscellaneous Materials

Anderson, Cordelia. *The Sport in Me* (activity book for ages 3-7). Order through The Children's Trust Fund, 444 Lafayette Rd. North, St. Paul, MN 55155-3839.

Child Abuse and Youth Sports: A comprehensive Risk Management Program (guide, video, brochures, booklets, training aids, awareness poster). Order through: National Institute for Youth Sports Administration, 2050 Vista Parkway, West Palm Beach, FL 33411, phone: 800-729-2057.

It's Not OK to Bully (video and coloring book). Order through Hazelton Educational Materials, 15251 Pleasant Valley Road, P. O. Box 176, Center City, MN 55012-1331, phone: 800-328-9000.

Kids and Company: Together for Safety. Program developed by the National Center for Missing and Exploited Children, 2101 Wilson Blvd., Suite 550, Arlington, VA 22201. Curriculum and teacher's guides available.

Appendix K
Organizational Resources Related to Child Sexual Abuse Prevention, Intervention, or Treatment

National Resource Center on Child Sexual Abuse of the National Center on Child Abuse and Neglect
107 Lincoln Street
Huntsville, AL 35801
205-534-6868
800-543-7006

King County Sexual Assault Resource Center
P. O. Box 300
Renton, WA 98057
206-226-5062

ETR Associates
P. O. Box 1830
Santa Cruz, CA 95061-1830
408-438-4060/800-321-4407
Fax: 408-438-4238

Channing L. Bete Co., Inc.
Scriptographic Booklets
200 State Road
South Deerfield, MA 01373
800-628-7733

National Committee to Prevent Child Abuse
332 S. Michigan Avenue, Suite 1600
Chicago, IL 60604
312-663-3520

National Committee to Prevent Child Abuse and Fulfillment Center
200 State Road
South Deerfield, MA 01373-0200
800-835-2671

IOF Prevention of Child Abuse Fund
P. O. Box 919029
San Diego, CA 92191-9029
619-550-2000

Sunburst Communications
P. O. Box 40
Pleasantville, NY 10570-0040
800-431-1934

Illusion Theater
528 Hennepin Avenue, Suite 704
Minneapolis, MN 55403
612-339-4944
Fax: 612-337-8042

Kids Rights
10100 Park Cedar Drive
Charlotte, NC 28210
800-892-KIDS
Fax: 704-541-0113

Team Entertainment Education
861 E. Millbrook Way
Bountiful, UT 84010
800-233-2212

National Clearinghouse on Child
Abuse and Neglect
P. O. Box 1182
Washington, DC 20013-1182
800-394-3366

AIMS Media
9710 DeSoto Avenue
Chatsworth, CA 91311-4409
800-367-2467

Intermedia
1300 Dexter Avenue North
Suite 220
Seattle, WA 98109-8336

Lucerne Media
37 Ground Pine Road
Morris Plains, NJ 07950
800-341-2293

Delawareans United to Prevent
Child Abuse
124 CD Senatorial Drive
Wilmington, DE 19807
302-654-1102
Fax: 302-655-5761

Knox County Child Abuse
and Neglect Council
P. O. Box 561
Rockland, ME 04841
207-236-6040

Act for Kids
A Division of the Spokane Sexual
Assault Center
7 S. Howard, Suite 200
Spokane, WA 99204-0323
509-747-8224

Child Welfare League of America
440 First Street NW
Suite 310
Washington, DC 20001-2085
202-638-2952

Kansas Children's Service League
Child Abuse Prevention Division
715 SW 10th
Topeka, KS 66612
913-354-7738

Coronet/MTI Film and Video
Disney Educational Productions and
Learning Corporation of America
P. O. Box 2649
Columbus, OH 43216
800-621-2131

Committee for Children
172 20th Avenue
Seattle, WA 98122
206-322-5050

Select Media Educational Film and Video
477 Broome Street, Suite 42
New York, NY 10013
212-431-8923

Red Flag Green Flag Resources
Rape and Abuse Crisis Center
P. O. Box 2984
Fargo, ND 58108
800-627-3675

Perpetration Prevention Project
Kempe National Center; UCHSC
1205 Oneida Street
Denver, CO 80220
303-321-3963

Altschul Group Corporation
1560 Sherman Avenue, Suite 100
Evanston, IL 60201
800-421-2363
708-328-6700
Fax: 708-328-6706

Learning Publications, Inc.
P. O. Box 1338
Holmes Beach, FL 34218-1338
800-222-1525
941-778-6651
Fax: 941-778-6818

**The C. Henry Kempe National Center
for Prevention and Treatment of
Child Abuse and Neglect**
University of Colorado Health
Sciences Center
1205 Oneida Street
Denver, CO 80220
303-321-3963

Family Welfare Research Group
1950 Addison Street, Suite 104
Berkeley, CA 94704
510-643-7020

The Ounce of Prevention Fund
188 W. Randolph, Suite 2200
Chicago, IL 60601
312-853-6080

VideoNet
P. O. Box 70525
Seattle, WA 98107
206-632-2378

The American Legion
Americanism Child and Youth Division
P. O. Box 1055
Indianapolis, IN 46206
317-630-1212
Fax: 317-630-1223

Boy Scouts of America
National Office
Audiovisual Service
P. O. Box 152079
Irving, TX 75015-2079
214-580-2598

Child Care Publications
P. O. Box 12024
University Station
Gainesville, FL 32604
904-472-4654

The Kids on the Block, Inc.
9385-C Gerwig Lane
Columbia, MD 21046
410-290-9095

**Mental Health Association of
Greater Dallas County**
2929 Carlisle, Suite 350
Dallas, TX 75204
214-871-2420

KIDPOWER
P. O. Box 1212
Santa Cruz, CA 95061
408-426-4407

It's About Childhood
The Hindman Foundation, Inc.
49 Northwest 1st Street, Suite 6
Ontario, OR 97914
800-305-HOPE

Children's Self-Help Center
120 Montgomery, Suite 1430
San Francisco, CA 94104
415-553-8680

Big Brothers/Big Sisters of America
230 N. 13th Street
Philadelphia, PA 19107
215-567-7000
Fax: 215-567-0394

The Parent Child Center of Tulsa
1516 S. Boston
Tulsa, OK 74119
918-599-7999

Coalition for Children
P. O. Box 6304
Denver, CO 80206
800-320-1717
303-320-6321

National Center for Missing and Exploited Children (NCMEC)
Publications Department
2101 Wilson Blvd., Suite 550
Arlington, VA 22201
800-843-5678

National Crime Prevention Council
1700 K Street NW, Second Floor
Washington, DC 20006-6272

Child Abuse Prevention Coalition
10865 Grandview Drive
Building #20, Suite 2040
Overland Park, KS 66210
913-338-2272

The Self-Helper
UCLA
California Self-Help Center
405 Hilgard Avenue, 2349 Franz Hall
Los Angeles, CA 90024-1563

Incest Survivors Resource Network International
P.O. Box 7375
Las Cruces, NM 88006-7375

NOVA (National Organization for Victim Assistance)
717 D Street NW
Washington, DC 20004
202-393-NOVA

Winters Communication, Inc.
14740 Lake Magdalene Circle
Tampa, FL 33613-1708
813-264-7618
800-788-3147

Northeastern Wisconsin In-School Telecommunications
Newist-CESA 7 IS 1110
University of WI, Green Bay
Green Bay, WI 54311
414-465-2599
800-633-7445

Protective Behaviors, Inc.
214 N. Hamilton
Madison, WI 53703
608-256-4572

Incest Resources, Inc.
46 Pleasant Street
Cambridge, MA 02139

NOW Legal Defense and Education Fund
99 Hudson Street
New York, NY 10013

Incest Survivors Information Exchange (ISIE)
P. O. Box 3399
New Haven, CT 06515

VOICES in Action, Inc.
(Victims of Incest Can Emerge Survivors)
P. O. Box 148309
Chicago, IL 60614
312-327-1500

National Victim Center
309 West 7th Street, Suite 705
Fort Worth, TX 76102
817-877-3355

Bridgework Theater
113-1/2 East Lincoln Avenue
Goshen, IN 46526

Kitchener - Reese
Alyce Reese
212 North 3rd Avenue, Suite 320
Minneapolis, MN   55401
612-338-5350

Sensibilities, Inc.
Cordelia Anderson
4405 Garfield Avenue South
Minneapolis, MN 55409
612-824-6217

Juvenile Justice Clearing House
NCJRS Reference Dept.
P. O. Box 6000
Rockville, MD 20850
800-638-8736

PACER (Parent Advocacy Coalition for Educational Rights)
Child Abuse Prevention Coordinator
4826 Chicago Avenue
Minneapolis, MN 55417
612-827-2966